D1529145

UPON THIS ROCK

Scriptural roots of Catholic teaching

Chantal Epie

UPON THIS ROCK

Scriptural roots of Catholic teaching

SCEPTER

London – New York

This edition of *Upon this Rock* is published:
in England by Scepter, 1 Leopold Road, London W5 3PB; and
in the United States by Scepter Publishers Inc., 481 Main Street,
New Rochelle, N.Y. 10801;
in collaboration with Criterion Publishers, P.O. Box 53342, Ikoyi,
Lagos.
© Original by Chantal Epie, 1991.
© This edition – Scepter, 1991.

Nihil Obstat:
Very Rev Fr J. M. Chapuli, S.T.D.
Imprimatur:
Most Rev Dr A. O. Okogie,
Archbishop of Lagos
26 June 1991

British Library Cataloguing in Publication Data
Chantal Epie (1949 –)

Upon this Rock: Scriptural roots of Catholic teaching.

1. Christian doctrine. God

I. Title

262.8

ISBN 0 906138 31 X
Cover: *Christ Pantokrator*, Elias Moskos (Crete), 1653,
Recklinghausen Ikonen-Museum, Germany.

Cover design and typeset by KIP Intermedia, and printed in
Singapore.

Contents

Foreword

This book is addressed to Christians: it takes it for granted that the reader firmly believes that the Bible is inspired by God and free from error because it is God's Word.

Its purpose is to show the Church as it is depicted in the Bible, especially in the New Testament, and to help the reader draw his own conclusions as to where this very same Church is to be found now in modern times.

Those Christians who seek exclusively the guidance of Holy Scripture and adopt the principle of private interpretation of the Bible reject the concept of a Church as a visible society established by Christ, endowed with divine authority to govern and to teach (which is what the Catholic Church claims to be); they also reject the necessity of the Sacraments, the need of Confession for the forgiveness of sins, the devotion to saints etc.

Yet the Bible has a lot to say on all these topics. But do we, Christians, read it attentively? How many fervent Christians have ever noticed that Holy Scripture tells of the divine approval of such Catholic practices as devotion to saints and to relics of saints? How many know that the Bible says that not all God's Revelation is written within its pages? How many have paid attention to the Epistles of St. Peter in which the Holy Spirit tells us that Holy Scripture can be very difficult to understand and its meaning very easy to distort if one relies exclusively on private interpretation?

One objective of this study is to help Christians to read the Bible with an understanding of its full meaning, and consequently to discover, emerging from the pages of the Sacred Books, the Catholic Church as it is today, as it has been throughout the centuries following the work of Redemption carried out by Christ.

So this book has been written especially for Catholics who wish to strengthen their Faith by increasing their knowledge of the *biblical sources* of Revelation. But it is also addressed to all people of good will who wish to be better acquainted with what the Bible says concerning Christ's teachings and the life of the first Christians, the immediate disciples of Jesus and of the Apostles.

With this purpose in view, the scope of this book is necessarily limited. No attempt has been made to bring forward proofs from the solemn definitions of dogmas of Faith. In spite of their primordial importance, hardly any reference has been made to conciliar and papal documents; for a complete explanation of Christian doctrine, there are other more appropriate publications (see Appendix on recommended bibliography). This book only aims at presenting the *scriptural proofs* of the Church's teachings, by studying the biblical texts directly related to the institution of the Church by Christ, the action of the Holy Spirit in the Church, the forgiveness of sin, the Mother of the Redeemer and other points of Catholic doctrine. However, whenever they shed light on the sacred text, extra-biblical historical facts have been used to reinforce the scriptural proofs.

1

The Sources of Revelation

*Stand firm, then, brethren, and hold by
the traditions you have learned, in word
or in writing, from us* (2 Thess 2:14).

Oral preaching of the Good News

*Those who had been driven away spread
the Gospel as they went from place to
place* (Acts 8:4).

The part of the Bible which we call the New
Testament was not handed down to us from Heaven in
its written form. Christianity is not a written religion as
such, differing in this from Islam. Mohammed claimed
that an Angel had given him the Book of the Koran,
and from that moment he started his religious teaching;
not so in the case of Jesus Christ.

Jesus Himself never wrote a word on paper for us.
The only time He is known to have been writing, it was
in the dust of the ground (John 8:6). He was always
teaching verbally, travelling from village to village, and

he trained His apostles to do the same. By the time the Faith had spread to Damascus, then to the rest of Asia Minor, Greece and Rome, there was still nothing written down under the inspiration of the Holy Spirit.

The first Gospel to be recorded in writing was the one of St. Matthew. He wrote in Aramaic for the Jewish Christians of Palestine approximately in the year 50 A.D. This original version does not seem to have been used outside the Holy Land because, after the destruction of Jerusalem in the year 70 A.D., when the city was reduced to a pile of rubble and the Sacred Books were burnt, no copy of it could be found. There was, however, a Greek translation of this Gospel, and this is the version which we possess nowadays.* So for 20 years there was no written Gospel, and yet the Good News of the Lord Jesus had spread like fire throughout the Roman Empire.

St. Mark's Gospel was written around the year 60 A.D., St. Luke's was written after Mark's, but before the destruction of Jerusalem, and John was a very old man when he wrote his Gospel and Epistles, towards the end of the 1st century.

In two of his letters, the Apostle John states in

---

* We know this is a translation from an Aramaic original because the expressions used and the structure of sentences follow an Aramaic pattern of speech which is often quite awkward in the Greek language. Moreover, as a Jew writing to his compatriots, St. Matthew was naturally using his own language. There are also extra-biblical testimonies of the existence of this Aramaic version of Matthew.

nearly identical terms that he still has many things to say, but he does not want to put them down on paper and prefers to speak face to face (2 John 12; 3 John 13-14). In his Gospel, we read that *there is much else besides that Jesus did; if all of it were put in writing, I do not think the world itself would contain the books which would have to be written* (John 21:25). The Acts of the Apostles tell us that *throughout the course of forty days He had been appearing to them, and telling them about the Kingdom of God* (Acts 1:3); yet, what we can read about those forty days is very brief and sketchy.

So it appears clearly that there was a considerable part of the Lord's teachings, later taught in their turn by the Apostles, that was not written down and cannot therefore be found in the Bible. These teachings, however, were faithfully transmitted to the Christian communities. In his two letters to the Thessalonians, written between the years 50 and 52 A.D., at a time when only St. Matthew's Gospel existed, St. Paul bears witness to this oral teaching that has to be received as God's words: *This is why we give thanks to God unceasingly that, when we delivered the divine message to you, you recognised it for what it is, God's message, not man's* (1 Thess 2:13). And we must not forget his warning: *Stand firm, then, brethren, and hold by the traditions you have learned, in word or in writing, from us* (2 Thess 2:14).

If we want to be faithful to God's word, we have to accept both the written Revelation and this other part of Revelation that was handed down to us by word of mouth and preserved for all generations in the Tradition of the Church.

In conclusion, we can affirm that the Bible itself

says that not everything taught by Christ is written within its pages. In addition, it qualifies as God's message the oral teaching of the Apostles. As the Bible is the word of God, we can safely conclude that God has warned us that His Revelation is to be found not only in Holy Scripture, but also in the Tradition of the Church transmitted from generation to generation by word of mouth, then also in the writings of early Christians such as St. Polycarp, disciple of St. John, St. Ignatius of Antioch, St. Augustine etc. Obviously, there can be no contradiction between Holy Scripture and Tradition as both take their origin from the Revelation of the One True God.

How the Gospels came to be written

> *Many have been at pains to set forth the history of what time has brought to fulfilment among us, following the tradition of those first eye-witnesses who gave themselves up to the service of the word* (Luke 1:1-2).

The teachings of Jesus Christ spread by word of mouth through the preaching of the first Christians forced by persecution to scatter all over the Roman Empire. It is enough to read the first chapters of the Acts of the Apostles to see the zeal with which they announced the Good News (see Acts 8). Soon, there were Christian communities in all the towns of Judaea and Samaria, as well as in Syria, Cyprus, Turkey and Greece, not to mention Rome.

After many years the growing Church felt the need for a written account of the teachings of the Apostles, that would serve as a guideline to future generations and would greatly facilitate the exact transmission of Christ's message throughout the centuries. So the Apostle Matthew wrote his Gospel for the Jewish-Christian communities of Palestine. Mark, faithful disciple and helper of Peter, recorded what he had heard from the Prince of the Apostles. Later on Luke, companion of St. Paul, prepared his own account. And many years later, John wrote the Fourth Gospel, recounting many events that had been omitted by his predecessors and leaving out others that were already very well documented in the first three Gospels.

The written Gospels were not meant to be an exhaustive, detailed account of Jesus' life and teachings, but a summary of the Apostles' preaching. They are not a theological treatise, but a teaching aid, sufficiently succinct to be easily memorised. In those days private study of Holy Scripture was practically ruled out: many centuries would still have to pass before the invention of the printing press. Every new copy had to be painstakingly handwritten and was reserved for reading in church and for religious instruction.

Holy Scripture itself bears witness to the fact that the Gospels were a summarised account of Christ's life and teaching. The record of the apparitions of the risen Lord in the course of 40 days occupies 12 verses in the Gospel of St. Matthew, 7 in St. Mark's, 40 in St. Luke's and 42 in St. John's. If we bear in mind that St. Luke's story is only repeating with greater detail what St. Mark had already said, it is quite clear that the Gospel accounts are only a brief summary covering the essential points of Jesus' last instructions to His Apostles. As these concerned the establishment of God's kingdom (Acts 1:3), they were of the highest importance not only to Jesus' immediate hearers, but to all Christian generations.

From this it follows that the Gospels were short notes or summaries of the abundant teaching of the Apostles and were intended to be used, not on their own, but together with oral tradition in the light of the official teaching of the Church.

Bible, Tradition, and Teaching Authority of the Church

> *All authority in heaven and on earth, he said, has been given to me; you, therefore, must go out, making disciples of all nations, and baptising them in the name of the Father, and of the Son, and of the Holy Spirit, teaching them to observe all the commandments which I have given you. And behold I am with you all through the days that are coming, until the consummation of the world* (Matt 28:18-20).

After His Resurrection, Jesus transferred to His apostles the task that had been entrusted to Him by God the Father: *I came upon an errand from my Father, and now I am sending you in my turn* (John 20:21), He had already announced. Just before He ascended into heaven, He solemnly invested them with His own authority when commanding them to go and teach all nations (see Matt 28:18-20 above).

A comparison with human sciences can throw some light on the nature and the necessity of a teaching authority in the Church.

To expect to understand all about Christianity from the study of Holy Scripture alone would be like preparing for a Master's Degree with the only help of revision notes and flash cards. An example from university life can illustrate the complementary character of Bible, Tradition and Teaching Authority (also called 'Magisterium'). To obtain high grades in his final examinations, a student cannot be satisfied with summarised notes. He should attend lectures and consult reference books from the library, doing extensive reading to know what experts in that particular field of learning have to say on the subject. However, in the course of his study the student may come across a number of difficulties, failing to understand certain statements or being unable to follow the development of a line of thought. He needs to go to a lecturer for help, ask various questions on the exact meaning of what he has read. Only then will his summarised notes prove extremely useful as a memory aid.

The same happens in the case of religious knowledge. Holy Scripture forms the summarised notes. The Tradition of the Church can be found in the ancient writings of Christians who lived in the first five centuries, expounding the Faith or defending it against heresies. To solve possible difficulties of interpretation of the Sacred Texts or of understanding of the

Tradition, the Christian can rely on the guidance of the teaching authority of the Church.

The Bible itself warns us of the ease with which it can be misunderstood. In the Second Letter of St. Peter, where he explains why the Last Judgment is not necessarily to be expected immediately, we read: *Our beloved brother Paul, with the wisdom God has granted him, has written you a letter* in which, as in all his letters, he speaks of this. (Though indeed there are passages in them difficult to understand, and these, like the rest of scripture, are twisted into a wrong sense by ignorant and restless minds, to their own undoing.) For yourselves, beloved, be warned in time; do not be carried away by their rash errors and lose the firm foothold you have won* (2 Peter 3:15-17).

Before that the Apostle Peter, writing under the inspiration of the Holy Spirit, stated in unambiguous terms that, precisely because Holy Scripture was God's own revelation to mankind, its interpretation could not be left to each individual reader. *And now the word of prophets gives us more confidence than ever. It is with good reason that you are paying so much attention to that word; it will go on shining like a lamp in some darkened room, until the dawn breaks, and the day-star rises in your hearts. Yet always you must remember this, that no prophecy in scripture is the subject of private interpretation. It was never man's impulse, after all, that gave us prophecy; men gave it utterance, but they*

---

* possibly 2 Thessalonians

were men whom God had sanctified, carried away, as they spoke, by the Holy Spirit (2 Peter 1:19-21).

So once more, the Bible itself bears witness of its own dependence on a teaching authority in the Church.

Guidance of the Holy Spirit

> *It will be for him, the truth-giving spirit,*
> *when he comes, to guide you into all truth*
> (John 16:13).

Is every soul directly and infallibly led by the Holy Spirit to a true understanding of Holy Scripture?

Experience tells us that there are very many good, honest and sincere Christians belonging to a number of Christian denominations, who read the Bible with devotion, and yet come out with very different, often contradictory, interpretations.

Let us consider the case of a Catholic and a Protestant who are reading Matt 16:12-20. The former understands it as the solemn promise by Christ to give Peter and his successors full authority over His Church. The latter attaches no such meaning to it, considering that Christ is pointing at Himself as the rock upon which He will build His Church, therefore giving no special importance to Peter.

If both interpretations are right, then God contradicts Himself, which is unthinkable. If one of the parties is wrong, then there is no infallible interpretation of Holy Scripture on the part of every individual Christian.

If the Catholic's interpretation is wrong, then

many generations of Christians in the course of
centuries, from the very beginning of the life of the
Church, found themselves deprived of the Holy Spirit's
guidance and fell into grave error, which is contrary to
Jesus' promise. There is abundant historical evidence
that Christians of the very first centuries already
looked upon the Bishops of Rome, successors of St.
Peter, as the Supreme Authority in the Church. Is it
reasonable to think that God would have allowed His
Church to err in such a point?

If, on the other hand, we accept the Bible's
testimony and acknowledge the existence of a Tradition
and of a Teaching Authority in the Church, then the
problem is solved. God's special assistance was
promised to this teaching authority, so that every
individual could always turn to it for guidance in his
search for the Truth. There is no contradiction between
Jesus' promise of light and the variety of
interpretations we find among sincere Christians. The
light of the Holy Spirit is equally available to all; the
only thing needed is 'to switch on the light', i.e. to
consult the teaching of the Church. To refuse to do so
is to prefer the twilight of our poor human
understanding, confusing it with the bright illumination
of the Holy Spirit.

Jesus in His Church offers His help to all alike. As
He did with the disciples of Emmaus, He continues
passing by, though not always in the way we would have
expected. But if we recognise Him in His Church, we
also shall exclaim: *Were not our hearts burning within us
when he spoke to us on the road, and when he made the
scriptures plain to us?* (Luke 24:32)

2

The Church established by Jesus Christ

... and it is upon this rock that I shall build my Church, and the gates of hell shall not prevail against it (Matt. 16:18).

Second Calling of the Twelve

He went out on to the mountain side, and passed the whole night offering prayer to God; and when day dawned, he called his disciples to him, choosing out twelve of them; these he called his apostles. Their names were Simon, also called Peter, his brother Andrew, James and John, Philip and Bartholomew, Matthew and Thomas, James the son of Alphaeus, and Simon who is called the zealot, Jude the brother of James, and Judas Iscariot, the man who turned traitor (Luke 6:12-16).

At the beginning of His public ministry, Jesus had called a number of men to follow Him. The Gospel recorded this first calling of Peter and Andrew, James and John (Matt. 4:18-22; Mark 1:16-20; Luke 5:9-11). John added more details about the vocation to follow Christ of himself, Andrew, Peter, Philip, Bartholomew also called Nathanael (John 1:35-51). Matthew told the story of his own calling (Matt 9:9-13), echoed by Mark and Luke (Mark 2:14-17; Luke 5:27-32).

But we read in St. Mark's Gospel that, later on, Jesus appointed twelve of his disciples for a special task. *And he went up on to the mountain side, and called to him those whom it pleased him to call; so these came to him, and he appointed twelve to be his companions, and to go out preaching at his command: to Simon he gave the fresh name of Peter; to James the son of Zebedee and his brother John, he gave the fresh name of Boanerges, that is, Sons of Thunder. The others were Andrew, and Philip, and Bartholomew, and Matthew, and Thomas, and James the son of Alphaeus, and Thaddaeus, and Simon the Cananean, and Judas Iscariot, the traitor* (Mark 3:13-19).

St. Luke tells us that Jesus chose twelve disciples after having spent the whole night in prayer. In such circumstances, this second *choice* or *call* of twelve men whose names are carefully recorded four times in the New Testament,* acquired a special solemnity that is

---

* cf. Matt. 10:2-4; Mark 3:16-19; Luke 6:14-16; Acts 1:13 (omitting Judas' name for obvious reasons)

understandable only if it signifies a new, special mission distinct from that of other ordinary followers of Christ.

The Gospels and the Acts of the Apostles make mention of *the Twelve* as a specific group well known to all (see Luke 9:12; Mark 6:7; 14:10; 14:17; John 6:68; 20:24; Acts 6:2). They were evidently a select group occupying a special position among Jesus' disciples.

Official witnesses of the Resurrection

> *There are men who have walked in our company all through the time when the Lord Jesus came and went among us, from the time when John used to baptise to the day when he, Jesus, was taken from us. One of these ought to be added to our number as a witness of his resurrection ... And the lot fell upon Matthias, and he took rank with the eleven apostles* (Acts 1:21-22:26).

During the Last Supper Jesus told the Twelve: *He whom I will send you from the Father's side, he will bear witness of what I was; and you are to be my witnesses, you who from the first have been in my company* (John 15:26-27). Just before ascending into heaven, He repeated: *You are to be my witnesses in Jerusalem and throughout Judaea, in Samaria, yes, and to the ends of the world* (Acts 1:8).

Soon afterwards, before the Holy Spirit had come down upon them, Peter proposed to cast lots to choose another apostle to replace Judas the traitor. The reason Peter gives is worth considering: *one of these ought to be added to our number as a witness of his resurrection* (Acts 1:22).

We know that the eleven remaining Apostles were not the only ones who had seen the risen Christ. True, the testimony of women had no legal value among Jews; therefore the Holy Women could not be considered as witnesses of the Resurrection. But Jesus had shown Himself to many disciples (though not to the world at large). There were Cleophas and his companion on the road to Emmaus (Luke 24:13-35), Matthias and Joseph Barsabas (Acts 1:21-23), and more than 500 disciples (1 Cor. 15:5-6). So why the need of adding a twelfth person to replace Judas and be counted among the Apostles as a witness of Jesus' Resurrection, when there were already so many witnesses?

There is only one satisfactory explanation. The Twelve had been appointed by Jesus Christ as his official witnesses. The 500 disciples, as well as Mary Magdalen, Joanna, Mary and the other women who saw the risen Saviour would certainly bear witness to it privately, among their friends and acquaintances. But only the Apostles were entitled to speak and act officially in the name of Jesus; they were Christ's ambassadors (2 Cor. 5:20), his accredited representatives on earth. When Cleophas or Joseph Barsabas spoke of the Resurrection, their testimony was that of a Christian; when the Apostles spoke, their testimony was that of the Church.

When God gives a Name

> *Jesus looked at him closely and said: thou art Simon the son of Jona; thou shalt be called Cephas (which means the same as Peter)* (John 1:42).

The Bible tells of special occasions when God Himself named a person. He named the first man Adam, which means 'man', making a play on words with 'adamah', a Hebrew word meaning 'earth'. *Man and woman both he created them, and gave them his blessing; and Adam was the name by which he called them at the time when they were first created* (Gen. 5:2). But the divine play on words also expressed a truth about man, whom God put in command of the whole earth and all that it contains (cf. Gen. 1:26) and placed in the Garden of Eden so that he would cultivate the land (cf. Gen. 2:15).

God changed Abram's name to Abraham, meaning 'father of a multitude', when He made a solemn covenant with him, promising to bless his descendants generation after generation. *And God said to him: I AM, and here is the covenant I make with thee, thou shalt be the father of a multitude of nations. No longer shall thy name be Abram, thou shalt be called Abraham, the father of a throng, such is the multitude of nations I will give thee for thy children* (Gen. 17:4-5).

Years later, God changed Jacob's name to 'Israel', renewing the promise already made to Abraham and Isaac. *Once again God revealed himself to Jacob, after his return from Mesopotamia of the Syrians, blessing him and assuring him, Thou shalt not be called Jacob any longer; Israel is to be thy name. So calling him by this name of Israel, he said to him: I am God all-powerful, and I bid thee increase and multiply; peoples shall descend from thee, whole families of nations, and kings shall be born of thy stock* (Gen. 35:9-11).

Indeed, when God gives a name, it is a meaningful one that actually expresses a reality, for God's word is all-powerful. Adam was the first father of the whole human race, made by God from the clay of the ground. Abraham became the father of a great multitude, and the children of his grandson Jacob became the patriarchs of the twelve tribes of Israel, the Chosen People.

When the time for our redemption arrived, God sent the Precursor of His Son, whose coming was heralded by an angel, as had happened before in the case of the great Samson (Judges 13). But this time God Himself chose the name of the last of the Old Testament prophets: *Thy wife Elizabeth is to bear thee a son, to whom thou shalt give the name of John* (Luke 1:14), a name which means 'God is gracious'. Indeed, John the Baptist's arrival in this world was a sign of God's graciousness towards men, and John was destined to prepare the way for the Saviour through whom man would be reconciled with God.

Then, *God sent the angel Gabriel to a city of Galilee called Nazareth, where a virgin dwelt, betrothed to a man of David's lineage* (Luke 1:26). The angel delivered God's message of salvation to Mary: *Behold, thou shalt conceive in thy womb, and shalt bear a son, and shalt call him Jesus* (Luke 1:31). The name 'Jesus' means 'God saves', and more than ever we see how effective God's word is. When He created the world,

His word was sufficient: *then God said, Let there be light; and the light began* (Gen. 1:3). The name given by God to His Only Begotten Son made man shows us clearly that Jesus is the Saviour, as was confirmed to Joseph a few months later: *and she will bear a son, whom thou shalt call Jesus, for he is to save his people from their sins* (Matt. 1:21).

It is in this context that we must listen to the Lord's words addressed to Andrew's brother Simon. *Jesus looked at him closely and said: thou art Simon the son of Jona; thou shalt be called Cephas* (*which means the same as Peter*) (John 1:42). The name Peter comes from the Greek πετρος, which means 'rock'.

Later on Jesus explained the full significance of that name, making a promise that reminds one of the solemn covenant God had made in ancient times with the patriarchs of the Old Testament: *Then Simon Peter answered, Thou art the Christ, the Son of the living God. And Jesus answered him: Blessed art thou, Simon Son of Jona; it is not flesh and blood, it is my Father in heaven that has revealed this to thee. And I tell thee this in my turn, that thou art Peter, and it is upon this rock that I will build my Church, and the gates of hell shall not prevail against it; and I will give to thee the keys of the kingdom of heaven; and whatever thou shalt bind on earth shall be bound in heaven; and whatever thou shalt loose on earth shall be loosed in heaven* (Matt. 16:16-19).

Strictly speaking Jesus did not change Simon's name but gave him a new title, which is no less significant. The title of *Rock* expressed a function Peter would have to fulfil. Jesus continued calling His Apostle Simon, but Simon was frequently referred to as

Simon the Rock (Simon Peter). Later on, when he actually assumed his function as Visible Head of the Church, he became more and more widely known as Peter.

The Rock, the foundation of the Church

> *Thou art Peter, and it is upon this rock that I shall build my Church* (Matt. 16:18).

Those intent on belittling the role of Peter and his successors in the Church affirm that Jesus used for naming Peter an aramaic word meaning 'small stone' while, pointing at Himself he added: *and upon this rock I shall build my Church*.†

Let us study what the original text of the Bible tells us.

We do not have the original aramaic version of St. Matthew's Gospel, but St. John, writing in Greek, preserved for us the exact word – Cephas – pronounced by Jesus: *thou shalt be called Cephas*‡

---

† Calvin was the first one to propose such interpretation, in the sixteenth century, in order to justify his separation from the Catholic Church. According to it, however, the whole Church would have misunderstood Jesus Christ's revelation and distorted the meaning of Holy Scriptures for more than 1,500 years, making ineffective the presence of the Holy Spirit in the Church and rendering valueless the promises of Christ.

‡ to be pronounced *Kefas*. The Aramaic word *Kefa* is written as *Cephas* in the Greek alphabet (an s was added in Greek to make the word sound masculine).

(which means the same as Peter) (John 1:42). This same name of Cephas was also used on several occasions by St. Paul (1 Cor. 1:12; Gal. 2:7; Gal 2:11; Gal 2:14).

There is no doubt at all that the word 'cephas' means rock. Now if we examine the Greek translation of St. Matthew's Gospel, we see that the name Πετρος (*Petros*) is attributed to Peter, while the word πετρα (*petra*) is used for the rock upon which Jesus would build His Church. The Greek dictionary tells us that both words mean the same thing: rock, or stone as a substance. The translator of the aramaic text chose the masculine form of πετρος as being more appropriate for a man's name, while he used the more common feminine form of πετρα for the foundation stone; the meaning is identical in both cases and the play on words is preserved by such translation of the one aramaic word 'cephas'. It happens also in other languages that several words can be used to indicate the same reality; in French, for example, there is no difference between the masculine word 'roc' and the feminine word 'roche', both meaning 'rock'.

The Bible itself bears witness to it. In all the passages where a piece of stone is mentioned, the inspired writer uses the Greek word λιθος (lithos): cf. Mark 5:5 (*crying aloud and cutting himself with stones*), Mark 13:2 (*Master, what stones! what a fabric!*), John 8:8 (*whichever of you is free from sin shall cast the first stone at her*), John 11:39 (*take away the stone, Jesus told them*). In the Greek translation of St. Matthew we also find λιθος for the stone the builders rejected (Matt. 21:42) and the stones used for the Temple buildings (Matt. 24:2).

By contrast, the word πετρα (petra) or its derivative πετρωδες (rocky) is used to indicate rock or stone as part of the crust of the earth: cf. Luke 6:48 (*he laid his foundation on rock*), Mark 4:5 and Matt. 13:5 (*and other seeds fell on rocky land, where the soil was shallow*), Matt. 27:51 (*and the earth shook and the rock parted asunder*).

It is very revealing to see how carefully St. Matthew's translator followed the original aramaic text of the Evangelist. When describing the burial of Jesus he shows clearly the difference between solid rock and a stone, no matter how big it might be: *Then he buried it in a new grave, which he had fashioned for himself out of the rock* (πετρα, *petra*), *and left it there, rolling a great stone* (λιθος, *lithos*) *against the grave door* (Matt. 27:60).*

If Jesus had called Andrew's brother 'small stone', St. Matthew's translator would have used the word λιθος (lithos) and Simon would not have been known as Peter by all Christian generations.

The Bible, therefore, proves beyond any reasonable doubt that Jesus intended Peter to be the rock upon which He would build His Church.

---

* This data can easily be verified in the New Testament published in Greek and Latin by the Catholic Book Agency, Via del Vaccaro 5, Rome.

The power of the keys

> *And I will give to thee the keys of the kingdom of heaven; and whatever thou shalt bind on earth shall be bound in heaven; and whatever thou shalt loose on earth shall be loosed in heaven* (Matt. 16:19).

Jesus made a solemn promise to Peter: that, in future, He would build His Church upon Peter, and that He would give him the keys of God's own kingdom. To hold the keys signifies to have authority. This appears very clearly in the Book of Isaias, when God promises to put Eliacim in charge of the Temple, for him *to rule all the citizens of Jerusalem, all Juda's race, with a father's care. I will give him the key of David's house to bear upon his shoulders; none may shut when he opens, none open when he shuts* (Isaias 22:22). So Christ was delegating to Peter His own authority, promising that Peter's decisions would be ratified in Heaven: *whatever thou shalt bind on earth will be bound in heaven; and whatever thou shalt loose on earth shall be loosed in heaven.*

Jesus therefore meant to give to Peter personally the authority and power He would bestow upon the Apostles as a group with His farewell words to the eleven disciples just before ascending into heaven: *all authority in heaven and on earth has been given to me; you, therefore, must go out, making disciples of all nations, and baptising them in the name of the Father, and of the Son, and of the Holy Spirit, teaching them to observe all the commandments which I have given you*

(Matt. 28:18-20). Earlier He had told them: *He who listens to you listens to me; he who despises you despises me; and he who despises me, despises him that sent me* (Luke 10:16), identifying Himself with the leaders of His Church.

When promising to Peter the keys of the kingdom of heaven, the Lord was making him His Representative, a promise that became effective after the Resurrection, when Jesus solemnly appointed Peter as Shepherd of His flock. *And when they had eaten, Jesus said to Simon Peter, Simon, son of John, dost thou care for me more than these others? Yes Lord, he told him, thou knowest well that I love thee. And he said to him, Feed my lambs. And again a second time he asked him, Simon, son of John, dost thou care for me? Yes, Lord, he told him, thou knowest well that I love thee. He said to him, Tend my shearlings. Then he asked him a third question, Simon, son of John, dost thou love me? Peter was deeply moved when he was asked a third time, Dost thou love me? and said to him, Lord, thou knowest all things; thou canst tell that I love thee. Jesus said to him, Feed my sheep* (John 21:15-17). Earlier, in Jerusalem, Jesus had declared: *I am the good shepherd* (John 10:11). After His Ascension into heaven, Peter was left to be the good shepherd, holding the keys of the sheepfold.

Jesus entrusted to Peter and the rest of the Apostles with him the power to teach (*you, therefore, must go out, making disciples of all nations*), to govern (*teaching them to observe all the commandments which I have given you*) and to sanctify men by sacred rites (*baptising them in the name of the Father, and of the Son, and of the Holy Spirit*). This power was conceded not only to themselves, but to all their successors throughout the centuries: *And behold I am with you all through the days that are coming, until the consummation of the world* (Matt. 28:20).

The Apostles understood in that way the words of the Lord. Even before Jesus left, they paid special deference to Peter. Peter always comes first on the list of the Apostles. When Jesus challenged the Twelve after his discourse on the Bread of Life, Peter speaks for them all: *Lord, to whom should we go? Thy words are the words of eternal life; we have learned to believe, and are assured that thou art the Christ, the Son of God* (John 6:69-70). After the Lord had ascended into heaven, Peter appears immediately in the *Acts of the Apostles* as the leader, interpreting authoritatively the Holy Scriptures (see Acts 1:15-26). On the day of Pentecost, when they are all filled with the Holy Spirit, Peter is their spokesman: *but Peter, with the eleven apostles at his side, stood there and raised his voice to speak to them* (Acts 2:14). Again, Peter appears as the authorised interpreter of Holy Scriptures (cf. Acts 2:15-36 and Acts 3:12-26). In the Council of Jerusalem gathered to decide the question of observances to be kept by Gentile converts, *there was much disputing over it, until Peter rose* (Acts 15:7); after listening to Peter, *then the whole company kept silence, and listened to Barnabas and Paul describing all the signs and wonders God had performed among the Gentiles by their means* (Acts 15:12).

God Himself wanted to respect this primacy of Peter over the rest of the Apostles. Although Divine Providence had chosen Paul to be the Apostle of the Gentiles, it was to Peter that God's intentions were first indicated, and he it was who first preached to the Gentiles and opened the doors of the Church to them (cf. the conversion of Cornelius, Acts, 10), convincing the apostles and brethren in Judaea: *Why then, they said, it seems God has granted life-giving repentance of heart to the Gentiles too* (Acts 11:18).

Of course, Jesus remains in the most proper sense the Rock, the Shepherd, the Teacher, the Judge, the King. But He delegated to Peter the task of administering His House, feeding His Flock, teaching His disciples, judging and ruling His People. Peter, with full delegated power, is *the faithful and wise steward, one whom his master will entrust with the care of the household, to give them their allowance of food at the appointed time: Blessed is that servant who is found doing this when his lord comes; I promise you, he will give him charge of all his goods* (Luke 12:42-44).

Peter's faith

> *And the Lord said: Simon, Simon, behold Satan has claimed power over you all, so that he can sift you like wheat: but I have prayed for thee, that thy faith may not fail; when, after a while, thou hast come back to me, it is for thee to be the support of thy brethren* (Luke 22:31-32).

From the very beginning, there was something special about Peter's faith. His profession of faith in Caesarea Philippi, *Thou art the Christ, the Son of the Living God* (Matt. 16:16) merited praise from Jesus.

And yet Peter was not the first to acknowledge Christ as the Son of God. Before him, Nathanael had made a similar act of faith: *Thou, Master, art the Son of God, thou art the King of Israel* (John 1:49). But Nathanael's recognition was based on human reasoning: *Jesus answered: What, believe because I told thee that I saw thee under the fig-tree? Thou shalt see greater things than that* (John 1:50). Peter's act of faith was something supernatural, fruit of God's grace: *And Jesus answered him: Blessed art thou, Simon son of Jona; it is not flesh and blood, it is my Father in heaven that has revealed this to thee* (Matt. 16:17).

Though his faith was still imperfect, Peter was the most daring of the Apostles in his trust in the Lord. When Jesus was seen in the midst of a storm, walking on the sea, the Apostles were terrified. But as soon as he heard Jesus' voice saying, *Take courage, do not be afraid*, Peter answered him, *Lord, if it is thyself, bid me come to thee over the water. He said, Come; and Peter let himself down out of the ship and walked over the water to reach Jesus* (Matt. 14:27-29). Then he wavered: *then, seeing how strong the wind was, he lost courage and began to sink.* A new act of faith and trust in the Lord: *whereupon he cried aloud, Lord, save me.* Jesus used that opportunity to strengthen Peter's faith: *and Jesus at once stretched out his hand and caught hold of him, saying to him: Why didst thou hesitate, man of little faith?* (cf. Matt. 14:26-33)

During the Last Supper, Jesus entrusted to Peter the task of strengthening the faith of the others. The devil, he said, is trying to overpower the Apostles and scatter them, *but I have prayed for thee, that thy faith may not fail* (Luke 22:32). Here it is important to preserve in English the difference between the way of addressing one person (thee) and the plural form (you). Jesus said: *Simon, Simon, behold Satan has claimed power over you all, so that he can sift you like wheat* (referring to the Apostles as a group), *but I have prayed for thee, that thy faith may not fail* (referring to Peter personally).

We know how all-powerful Jesus' prayer is. He told us so when raising Lazarus from the dead: *and Jesus lifted his eyes to heaven, Father, he said, I thank thee for hearing my prayer. For myself, I know that thou hearest me at all times, but I say this for the sake of the multitude which is standing round, that they may learn to believe it is thou who hast sent me* (John 11:41-42).

As Jesus prayed for Peter's faith not to fail, we can be sure that Peter's faith will remain unshakeable, like rock. Jesus knew well that Peter would deny him, but He saw farther ahead. He knew Peter would come back to Him, and He counted on him as the rock upon which He would build His Church: *when, after a while, thou hast come back to me, it is for thee to be the support of thy brethren* (Luke 22:32).

Evidently, Jesus was not establishing His Church only for the lifetime of the Apostles. He meant it to last till the end of the world. Therefore the rock had to remain as long as the Church existed, and Peter's role would be maintained throughout the ages. Peter's successors continue to be an infallible guide for all Christians, as infallible as Jesus' prayer that his faith might not fail.

Peter's weaknesses and God's power

> *The Lord told me, 'My grace is enough for thee; my strength finds its full scope in thy weakness'. More than ever, then, I delight to boast of the weaknesses that humiliate me, so that the strength of Christ may enshrine itself in me* (2 Cor. 12:9).

Peter's weaknesses were undeniable. He was very spontaneous, and his impetuosity was often the result of thoughtlessness. He was stronger in his words than in his deeds. Yet he was sincere, transparent in his simplicity. The Lord knew very well all his defects, but *He whose power is at work in us is powerful enough, and more than powerful enough, to carry out his purpose beyond all our hopes and dreams* (Eph. 3:20).

It is in St. Mark's Gospel that we read more anecdotes showing Peter in an unfavourable light, and Mark was precisely transmitting what he had heard from St. Peter himself. It is clear that Peter had learned the lessons of his Master; he did not put his trust in himself but in the Lord, and did not try to 'put on a good appearance'. St. Mark tells us about Jesus rebuking Peter: *but he turned about and, seeing his disciples there, rebuked Peter; Back, Satan, he said, these thoughts of thine are man's, not God's* (Mark 8:33). We are told of Peter's cowardice and of his denial of Jesus (Mark 14:50-72), and of his incapacity to watch with his Master: *and he said to Peter: Simon, art thou sleeping? Hadst thou not strength to watch even for an hour?* (Mark 14:37).

Even many years later, Peter showed signs of weakness, not in his faith, but in his behaviour, when he kept away from Gentiles in the presence of the supporters of circumcision. St. Paul reproved him with strong words (cf. Gal 2:11-14). Certainly Peter, on that specific occasion, was not practising what he taught. When meeting the centurion Cornelius he had exclaimed: *I see clearly enough that God makes no distinction between man and man; he welcomes anybody, whatever his race, who fears him and does what piety demands* (Acts 10:35). In the Council of Jerusalem he had spoken in favour of the Gentiles: *God would not make any difference between us and them; he had removed all the uncleanness from their hearts when he gave them faith* (Acts 15:9). He had approved the Council's decree: *It is the Holy Spirit's pleasure and ours that no burden should be laid upon you beyond these, which cannot be avoided; you are to abstain from what is sacrificed to idols, from blood-meat and meat which has been strangled, and from fornication. If you keep away from such things, you will have done your part. Farewell* (Acts 15:28-29). So St. Paul censured Peter's behaviour, but there is nothing to show that he questioned his authority.

A common objection to Peter's infallible teaching and supreme authority in the Church is the historical evidence of some great sinners among Peter's successors, the Bishops of Rome. In this respect it is suitable to point out that: 1) the number of such unworthy Popes is very small compared to the number of holy men who occupied Peter's Chair; 2) even those unworthy leaders of the Church never taught anything contrary to Faith and Morals; they knew their own sinfulness and never tried to teach that their evil deeds were good or to distort the Christian Creed.

In addition, the Bible has preserved for us Jesus Christ's command to obey the lawful religious authorities, independently from their own personal worthiness. When condemning the hypocrisy of the scribes and pharisees, the Lord reaffirmed their authority to teach and their right to be obeyed: *The Scribes and Pharisees, he said, have established themselves in the place from which Moses used to teach; do what they tell you, then, continue to observe what they tell you, but do not imitate their actions, for they tell you one thing and do another* (Matt. 23:2-3).

Peter was well aware of his responsibility to live according to the demands of his vocation, and he taught others to do the same. *Bestir yourselves then, brethren, ever more eagerly, to ratify God's calling and choice of you by a life well lived* (2 Peter 1:10). He fully shouldered the weight of the charge laid upon him by the Lord Jesus Christ, of being a support for his brethren. *And now I have a charge to give to the presbyters in your company; I, who am a presbyter like themselves, I, who bear witness of Christ's sufferings, I, who have my part in that glory which will one day be revealed. Be shepherds to the flock God has given you. Carry out your charge as God would have it done, cordially, not like drudges, generously, not in the hope of sordid gain; not tyrannizing, each in his own sphere, but setting an example, as best you may, to the flock. So, when the Prince of shepherds makes himself known, your prize will be that crown of glory which cannot fade. And you, who are young, must defer to these, your seniors* (1 Peter 5:1-5).

The Apostles, ministers of Christ, Shepherds of the Church

> *From Miletus he sent a message to Ephesus, summoning the presbyters of the Church there. And when they had come out to him and gathered round him, he said to them: ... I have never shrunk from revealing to you the whole of God's plan. Keep watch, then, over yourselves and over God's Church, in which the Holy Spirit has made you bishops; you are to be the shepherds of that flock which he won for himself at the price of his own blood* (Acts 20:17-18, 27-28).

Jesus established His Church upon the foundation of the twelve Apostles. So does the Apocalypse (also called Book of Revelation) describe the *bride, whose bridegroom is the Lamb* which is the Heavenly Jerusalem, i.e. God's Church: *The city wall, too, had twelve foundation-stones; and these, too, bore names, those of the Lamb's twelve apostles* (Apoc. 21:14). And St. Paul tells the Ephesians: *Apostles and prophets are the foundation on which you were built, and the chief corner-stone of it is Jesus Christ himself* (Eph. 2:20).

In His discourse at the Last Supper, Jesus had promised His Apostles authority over His Church: *You are the men who have kept to my side in my hours of trial: and, as my Father has allotted a kingdom to me, so I allot to you a place to eat and drink at my table in my kingdom; you shall sit on twelve thrones, judging the twelve tribes of Israel* (Luke 22:28-30). The term 'judging' is equivalent to 'ruling' and evokes the era of the Judges of Israel (see Book of Judges).

The Apostles have authority to judge and to punish members of the Church who do not act according to God's will. Peter judged Ananias and his wife Sapphira (Acts 5:1-10). Paul ordered the expulsion of a man guilty of grave sin: *Why, there are reports of incontinence among you, and such incontinence as is not practised even among the heathen; a man taking to himself his father's wife. And you, it seems, have been contumacious over it, instead of deploring it, and expelling the man who has been guilty of such a deed from your company. For myself, though I am not with you in person, I am with you in spirit; and, so present with you, I have already passed sentence on the man who has acted thus. Call an assembly, at which I will be present in spirit, with all the power of Our Lord Jesus Christ, and so, in the name of Our Lord Jesus Christ, hand over the person named to Satan, for the overthrow of his corrupt nature, so that his spirit may find salvation in the day of Our Lord Jesus Christ* (1 Cor. 5:1-5).*

To understand better how the leaders of today's Church can still be invested with divine authority, it is interesting to see how, right from the beginning, new appointments to positions of government in the Church had both a human and a supernatural element, so that

---

* The last words indicate the corrective nature of the punishment; it is hoped that the severity of the sentence will bring about the repentance of the sinner.

they were made by men, and yet were ratified by God.
The election of Matthias as an Apostle is a clear
example of this: Peter made a proposal, the assembly
of the disciples named two candidates, using their own
judgement to select the best qualified persons, and
then they prayed for God to make the final choice
through the casting of lots (cf. Acts 1:15-26); it would
have made no difference to God's freedom of choice if
they had voted by secret ballot. The very direct
intervention of God in the appointment of Paul and
Barnabas was the exception rather than the rule (cf.
Acts 13:2-3). The Acts tell us how, having founded new
Christian communities in Lystra, Iconium and Antioch,
*with fasting and prayer they appointed presbyters for
them in each of the churches, and commended them to
the care of the Lord in whom they had learned to believe*
(Acts 14:22).

St. Paul attributes such appointments to Christ,
who *has appointed some to be apostles, others to be
prophets, others to be evangelists, or pastors, or teachers.
They are to order to lives of the faithful, minister to their
needs, build up the frame of Christ's body, until we all
realize our common unity through Faith in the Son of
God, and fuller knowledge of Him* (Eph. 4:11-13). And
the same Apostle of the Gentiles did not hesitate to
declare to the leaders of the Christian community of
Ephesus: *Keep watch, then, over yourselves and over
God's Church, in which the Holy Spirit has made you
bishops* (Acts 20:28).

The Bible testifies that the Apostles and their
successors were not carrying out a human task, but a
divine ministry. *So much I owe to the grace which God
has given me, in making me a priest of Jesus Christ for*

the Gentiles, with God's Gospel as my priestly charge, to make the Gentiles an offering worthy of acceptance, consecrated by the Holy Spirit (Rom. 15:16). And *we sent our brother Timothy, who exercises God's ministry in preaching the Gospel of Christ, to confirm your resolution and give you the encouragement your Faith needs* (1 Thess. 3:2).

This priestly ministry, bestowed by God Himself, is to be transmitted to others according to the needs of the Church. *It is for you to appoint presbyters, as I enjoined, in each city, always looking for a man who is beyond reproach ...* (Titus 1:5-6). It is evident that, although the Holy Spirit makes a man a bishop (cf. Acts 20:28), the actual appointment is made by men, and therefore St. Paul insists on the conditions of selection of the shepherds of the Church: *A bishop, after all, since he is the steward of God's house, must needs be beyond reproach. He must not be an obstinate or quarrelsome man, one who drinks deep, or comes to blows, or is grasping over money. He must be hospitable, kindly, discreet, upright, unworldly, continent* (Titus 1:7-8; see also 1 Tim. 3:1-7).

The pastors of the Church, consecrated by God Himself, have a position of authority and obedience is due to them. *Obey those who have charge of you, and yield to their will; they are keeping unwearied watch over your souls, because they know they will have an account to give* (Heb. 13-17). It is clear, therefore, that they are responsible for guiding the Christian people on the paths of holiness; they are responsible for the salvation of their souls and have the grave duty of governing them according to God's plans. The Christian people have the corresponding obligation of honouring them and obeying them. *Brethren, we would ask you to pay deference to those who work among you, those who have charge of you in the Lord, and give you directions; make it a rule of charity to hold them in special esteem, in honour of the duty they perform, and maintain the unity with them* (1 Thess. 5:12-13).

The Church's hierarchical structure

The Acts of the Apostles as well as the Epistles show that the government of the Church was organised according to a hierarchical structure wanted by God.

We have already seen Peter's leading role. The other Apostles, in union with Peter, had authority to govern the Church. They could be assisted by others, to whom they delegated part of their tasks.

When they saw the need of having helpers for carrying out works of mercy, *the Twelve called together the general body of the disciples* and told them to select *seven men who are well spoken of, full of the Holy Spirit and of wisdom; and they chose Stephen, a man who was full of faith and of the Holy Spirit, Philip, Prochorus, Nicanor, Timon, Parmenas, and Nicolaus, who was a proselyte from Antioch. These they presented to the apostles, who laid their hands on them with prayer* (Acts 6:1-6).

When there was a controversy in Antioch about the necessity of circumcision for the Gentiles converted to Christianity, the matter was taken to the central governing body of the Church. *It was decided that Paul and Barnabas and certain of the rest should go up to see the apostles and presbyters in Jerusalem about this question* (Acts 15:2). The wording of the decree adopted by this first Council reflects God's very special action in the government of His Church: *It is the Holy Spirit's pleasure and ours that no burden should be laid upon you beyond these ...* (Acts 15:28). The whole Church, not only the Christians of Antioch, were bound by that decision; the Acts tell us that Paul *travelled all through Syria and Cilicia, establishing the churches in the faith, and bidding them observe the commands which the apostles and presbyters had given* (Acts 15:41).

This power of government belonged exclusively to Peter and the other Apostles, and to those appointed by them as their successors. No other self-appointed authority, no matter how well-intentioned it was, could interfere with the divinely established organization of the Church. This is why, in the decree promulgated by the Apostles and presbyters in the first Council ever to be celebrated in the Church, we read: *We hear that some of our number who visited you have disquieted you by what they said, unsettling your consciences, although we had given them no such commission. And therefore, meeting together with common purpose of heart, we have resolved to send you chosen messengers, in company with our beloved Barnabas and Paul, men who have staked their lives for the name of Our lord Jesus Christ. We have given this commission to Judas and Silas, who will confirm the message by word of mouth* (Acts 15:24-27).

The only authorised official representatives of Jesus Christ on earth are the successors of the apostles (all the bishops led by the Bishop of Rome),* helped by

---

* St. Peter, at first, remained in the land of Israel. Soon he moved to Antioch. Later on he established the seat of his authority in Rome, the capital of the Roman Empire. He remained Bishop of Rome for 15 to 20 years until his death by crucifixion.

priests and deacons, consecrated according to the rite used in the first place by the Apostles themselves, and continued by their successors throughout the centuries. Such consecration was done through the imposition of the hands of an Apostle, or a bishop (cf. the consecration of deacons, Acts 6:6; of bishops and priests, 1 Tim. 4:14; 1 Tim. 5:22). And St. Paul warns Timothy of his grave responsibility in transmitting to others the power of government: *As for the imposition of hands, do not bestow it inconsiderately, and so share the blame for the sins of others* (1 Tim. 5:22).

The Church, pillar and foundation of truth

> ... *so that, if I am slow in coming, thou mayest be in no doubt over the conduct that is expected of thee in God's household. By that I mean the Church of the living God, the pillar and foundation upon which the truth rests* (1 Tim. 3:15).

The two Epistles of St. Paul to Timothy and the Epistle to Titus are sometimes called 'Pastoral Epistles' because they are addressed to these two men, not as members of the Church at large but in their capacity as Shepherds of Christ's Flock. The three letters make reference to their responsibility as leaders and teachers of their respective Christian communities.

In the Pastoral Epistles, a strong emphasis is laid on the importance of sound doctrine, of truth. An attentive study of these texts shows that St. Paul is not speaking of purely subjective truths liable to vary according to persons and times. On the contrary, he warns against such variations, insisting on the bishop's duty to remain faithful to apostolic teachings. *With all the faith and love thou hast in Christ Jesus, keep to the pattern of sound doctrine thou hast learned from my lips. By the power of the Holy Spirit who dwells in us, be true to thy high trust* (2 Tim. 1:13-14).

There are bound to be attacks against the truth, he explains. Moses suffered from them, and so will all those entrusted by God to teach the truth (cfr. 2 Tim. 3:8). *The time will surely come, when men will grow tired of sound doctrine, always itching to hear something fresh; and so they will provide themselves with a continuous succession of new teachers, as the whim takes them, turning a deaf ear to the truth, bestowing their attention on fables instead* (2 Tim. 4:3-4). But the bishop must stand firm, carrying out his teaching work and keeping the doctrine unaltered in spite of people's desire for change. *It is for thee to be on the watch, to accept every hardship, to employ thyself in preaching the gospel, and perform every duty of thy office, keeping a sober mind* (2 Tim. 4:5).

Such an effort on the part of the bishop to preserve Christ's teachings from human distortions means that there is no such thing as a purely subjective truth for Christians. There is only one truth, witnessed to by Christ. The Lord referred to it in His brief conversation with Pilate. *What I was born for, what I came into the world for, is to bear witness of the truth. Whoever belongs to the truth, listens to my voice* (John 18:37). These words evoke another statement of Jesus to His Apostles: *he who listens to you, listens to me* (Luke 10:16).

In other words, Christians are to seek the Truth in the teachings of Christ entrusted for safekeeping to the Apostles and their successors, the bishops of the Church. This is where the expression 'deposit of the Faith' comes from. Jesus Christ entrusted the Truth to His Apostles for the benefit of the whole Church, not for them to do as they pleased with it, but for safekeeping. At the end of time the last successors of the Apostles, in union with the last Pope and surrounded by the whole People of God, will be expected to possess this sacred deposit in all its integrity.

There is another significant point in Jesus' words to Pilate. *Whoever belongs to the truth* ... He says. If I belong to the truth, the truth must have a reality of its own outside me. If truth is only the product of my own mind, something I forge for myself to satisfy my subjective needs, then the truth belongs to me, but I cannot properly say that I belong to the truth.

The idea of a purely subjective truth is not new. To Jesus' affirmation of one Truth, Pilate reacted with a shrug. *Pilate said to him, What is truth? And with that he went back to the Jews again* (John 18:38) without waiting for an answer. This episode illustrates the consequences of subjectivism with regard to Christ. It was most inconvenient for Pilate to arouse the anger of the Jews; he therefore adapted his reasoning to suit his own subjective good. At the same time as he declared: *I have no part in the death of this innocent man; it concerns you only* (Matt. 27:24), he used his authority as governor to condemn Christ to death. He actually convinced himself he was free from all blame for Jesus' death. Subjectively he felt innocent; objectively he was guilty of criminal injustice and cowardice. A similar danger threatens those who affirm *Christ is my Lord and Saviour* while despising the teaching authority of those appointed by Christ *to minister this reconciliation of his to others* (2 Cor. 5:18).

But is it possible for the teaching of the Church to remain unchanged throughout the centuries? Would this static approach not be a short-cut to stagnation? After all, doesn't the Catholic Church itself, for all its claims to infallibility, offer new teachings from time to time, defining new dogmas which must be believed by all Catholics?

To find the right answer to these vital questions it is necessary to distinguish between substantial change (either by addition or by elimination) and accidental change (by way of internal growth or development). Substantial change is radically opposed to fidelity to the teachings of Christ, as St. Paul repeatedly teaches in the Pastoral Epistles. Accidental change, however, takes place as Christians study those teachings, using their intellectual power to go deeper and deeper into their meaning. The development of theology brings about a greater depth of knowledge. The teachings of the Church seem to multiply, yet they are simply growing just as a tree grows from a tiny seed; the tree is contained in the seed, though considerable time has to elapse before it reaches its full growth. Dogmas are not new truths; they are old beliefs officially confirmed and defined by the Church to strengthen the Faith of the People of God.

This theological development is not the exclusive responsibility of the Governing Church. Indeed the Church owes a great deal to the work of research and study of theologians, many of whom have received the title of 'Doctors of the Church', and welcomes it as a manifestation of the vitality of the People of God. One cannot separate as two opposed realities the Teaching Church and the Mystical or Charismatic Church. There is only one Church: God's People, the great family of God's children, *God's household* (cfr. 1 Tim. 3:15). Within this household, different people are called to perform different functions. Any social structure includes some who govern and others who are governed; yet good government benefits the whole society, down to the very last of its members, respecting their legitimate freedom while protecting them from deceptions of all kinds.

With this in mind we can appreciate in all their significance the words of St. Paul to Timothy following the enumeration of the qualities to be possessed by bishops, priests and deacons. *So much I tell thee by letter, although I hope to pay thee a visit before long; so that, if I am slow in coming, thou mayest be in no doubt over the conduct that is expected of thee in God's household. By that I mean the Church of the living God, the pillar and foundation upon which the truth rests* (1 Tim. 3:14-15).

First, the Apostle makes a casual reference to the existence of an abundant oral Tradition; his words seem to imply that he generally preferred to speak rather than write, and used the written word only when he had no other means of communication.

Then he states the special responsibility of Timothy as a Shepherd of Christ's Flock, a Teacher, Judge and Leader of God's People. God dwells in His Church, and the Church possesses the Truth about

God. St. Paul's words recall the Lord's great promise to Peter. Peter had exclaimed: *Thou art the Christ, the Son of the living God* (Matt. 16:16) and Jesus had named him Rock. *It is upon this rock that I will build my church; and the gates of hell shall not prevail against it* (Matt. 16:18). Peter is the rock upon which God's house is built, the solid foundation that renders the house indestructible. *Then a flood came, and the river broke upon that house, but could not stir it; it was founded upon rock* (Luke 6:48). Every faithful Christian is a part of this building, but his strength does not lie in his own individual worth (what can be achieved with one isolated brick?). No, the value of a Christian's Faith lies in his union with Christ together with his brothers in the Faith taught by Christ, who is *the living antitype of that stone which men rejected, which God has chosen and prized; you too must be built up on him, stones that live and breathe, into a spiritual fabric* (1 Peter 2:4-5).

To be built on Christ is to follow the Apostles' teaching. This is confirmed by the words St. Paul had earlier written to the Ephesians. *You belong to God's household. Apostles and prophets are the foundation on which you were built, and the chief cornerstone of it is Jesus Christ himself. In him the whole fabric is bound together, as it grows into a temple, dedicated to the Lord; in him you too are being built in with the rest, so that God may find in you a dwelling-place for his Spirit* (Eph. 2:20-22). Union with the Apostles is presented as a condition for the presence of the Holy Spirit, the Spirit of Truth, in the Church.

The Mystical Church is a pillar and foundation upon which the truth rests because it is the House of

God built by Jesus Christ upon the rock of Peter. Shift it to another site, take it away from this rock, and you will be left with *a house in the earth without foundation; when the river broke upon it, it fell at once, and great was that house's ruin* (Luke 6:49).

Rebuild God's House away from Peter, and it will no longer be the Church of the living God, for then the gates of hell, i.e. the devil, will be able to prevail against it. The devil, remember, *is all false, and it was he who gave falsehood its birth* (cfr. John 8:44); moreover *he, from the first, was a murderer* (cfr. John 8:44). But Christ is Truth and Life (cfr. John 14:6).

Accept to be one of those living stones built upon Christ, the chief corner-stone represented by Peter the Rock, and you become, in union with the whole Church, a pillar of truth, a source of unerring knowledge for all who seek the Truth.

The Church, authentic interpreter of God's revelation

No prophecy in scripture is the subject of private interpretation (2 Peter 1:20).

The representatives of Christ in the Church are not to use their authority to serve their own whims and fancy, but to preserve the deposit of Faith intact throughout the centuries. Therefore they cannot change the contents of the Faith but must always respect the traditional teachings of their predecessors. St. Paul, writing under the inspiration of the Holy Spirit, speaks about it in no uncertain terms: *Friends, though it were we ourselves, though it were an angel from heaven that should preach to you a gospel other than the gospel we preached to you, a curse upon him! I repeat now the warning we gave you before it happened, if anyone preaches you what is contrary to the tradition you received, a curse upon him!* (Gal 1:8-9). So the Bible's testimony on the Church established by Jesus Christ is that there can be no contradiction between the teachings of the Church today and the teachings of the Church in apostolic times.

No prophecy in scripture is the subject of private interpretation, the Holy Spirit warns us through Peter (2 Peter 1:20). After all, the devil himself knows how to quote the Bible, interpreting selected passages to suit his own purpose. *Next the devil took him into the holy city, and there set him down on the pinnacle of the Temple, saying to him, If thou art the Son of God, cast thyself down to earth; for it is written, He has given charge to his angels concerning thee, and they will hold thee up with their hands, lest thou shouldst chance to trip on a stone* (Matt. 4:5-6). St. Peter warns us that, in the letters of St. Paul, *there are passages difficult to understand and these, like the rest of scriptures, are twisted into a wrong sense by ignorant and restless minds, to their own undoing* (2 Peter 3:16).

The interpretation of Sacred Scriptures belongs to the teaching authority of the Church, who alone can guarantee their true meaning, studying the Bible in the light of the traditional teaching of the Church. The Bishops of the Church *must hold firmly to the truths which have tradition for their warrant; able, therefore, to encourage sound doctrine and to show the wayward their error* (Titus 1:9).

3

The Sanctifying Action of the Holy Spirit: I – New Birth

John's Baptism was one of the rites of purification that was familiar to the Jewish people. It was a symbol of the washing away of sins and was meant to be an external manifestation of inner repentance. It did not actually bring about the forgiveness of sins and cleansing of the soul, but was a preparation for the eventual arrival of the Saviour who would indeed pour the treasures of God's grace upon those who believed in Him. *As for me, I am baptising you with water, for your repentance; but one is to come after me who is mightier than I, so that I am not worthy even to carry his shoes for him; he will baptise you with the Holy Spirit, and with fire* (Matt. 3:11).

Just before ascending into heaven, Jesus commanded His disciples *not to leave Jerusalem, but to wait there for the fulfilment of the Father's promise. You have heard it, he said, from my own lips; John's baptism, I told you, was with water, but there is a baptism with the Holy Spirit which you are to receive, not many days from this* (Acts 1:4-5).

A superficial reading of Sacred Scripture can give the impression that John's baptism and Christian baptism are opposed in such a way that in the latter the element of water would have been eliminated. As a consequence, we find certain non-baptised persons who, after some vivid spiritual experience, affirm that they have been baptised with the Holy Spirit and neglect to go through the Christian rite of Baptism.

We must keep in mind that no passage of the Bible should be considered in isolation from the rest of Scriptures. As God cannot contradict Himself, it is necessary to study all the passages dealing with the same topic, so that no single text may be interpreted in a way that is incompatible with another.

The Baptismal Rite in the early Church

> *See, there is water here; why may I not be baptised? Philip said, If thou dost believe with all thy heart, thou mayest. And he answered: I believe that Jesus Christ is the Son of God. So he had the chariot stopped, and both of them, Philip and the eunuch, went down into the water, and Philip baptised him there* (Acts 8:36-37).

When going carefully through the pages of the New Testament, one can observe that the word *baptism* used on its own always refers to a rite involving the use of water and to which the new convert submits himself voluntarily. If it is used in a different sense, then the word is qualified, i.e. the kind of baptism referred to is specified or at least implied. When the sons of Zebedee thoughtlessly requested the highest honours in the kingdom of God, Jesus asked them: *Have you strength to drink of the cup I am to drink of, to be baptised with the baptism I am to be baptised with? They said to him: We have. And Jesus told them, you shall indeed drink of the cup I am to drink of, and be baptised with the baptism I am to be baptised with* (Mark 10:38-39). There He meant a baptism of suffering. When reminding His apostles that they were to receive the Holy Spirit in all His power, He speaks of a *baptism with the Holy Spirit which you are to receive, not many days from this* (Acts 1:5).

So Jesus would baptise with the Holy Spirit. Yet when we read the Acts of the Apostles, we are forced to recognise the existence of a Baptism with water, distinct from the reception of the Holy Spirit that was sometimes – not necessarily – accompanied by extraordinary manifestations. After Philip the deacon had baptised the people of Samaria converted to the Lord, Peter and John went to see them *and prayed for them, that they might receive the Holy Spirit, who had not, as yet, come down on any of them; they had received nothing so far except baptism in the name of the Lord Jesus. Then the apostles began to lay their hands on them, so that the Holy Spirit was given them* (Acts 8:15-17). Years later, in Ephesus, Paul *met some disciples there and asked them: was the Holy Spirit given to you, when you learned to believe?* (Acts 19:1-2); evidently, reception of the Holy Spirit was not automatic upon finding faith in Jesus Christ. When they answered: *nobody even mentioned to us the existence of a Holy Spirit*, St. Paul understood that there was something wrong, as the command of the Lord had been clear and explicit: to make disciples of all nations, *baptising them in the name of the Father, and of the Son, and of the Holy Spirit* (Matt. 28:19). *What baptism, then, did you receive? Paul asked; and they said, John's baptism* (Acts 19:3). After speaking to them about faith in Jesus, *on hearing this, they received baptism in the name of the Lord Jesus; and when Paul laid his hands upon them, the Holy Spirit came down on them, and they spoke with tongues, and prophesied* (Acts 19:5-6).

So there was a Baptism, and there was a *laying on of hands*. The normal procedure was for a new convert to receive baptism. Only afterwards, as a second step, would the Holy Spirit come down upon him. On one occasion it did not happen in this way, but the sacred writer makes it clear that it was an exceptional case motivated, no doubt, by the extreme resistance of Jewish Christians to accept Gentiles in the Church. God intervened in a very special way to bring about the admission of Cornelius and his relatives and friends as members of the Church. When the Holy Spirit came upon them, Peter could do nothing else but allow them to be baptised; indeed, only such extraordinary manifestation of God's will was able to convince the rest of the Church: *And then, when I had set about speaking to them, the Holy Spirit fell upon them, just as it was with us at the beginning. Then I was reminded of what the Lord said to us, John's baptism was with water, but there is a baptism with the Holy Spirit which you are to receive. And now, if God has made them the same free gift, which he made to us when faith in the Lord Jesus had gone before it, who was I, what power had I, to stay God's hands? At these words they were content, and gave glory to God; why then, they said, it seems God has granted life-giving repentance of heart to the Gentiles too* (Acts 11:15-18).

Baptism with water and the Holy Spirit

> *Believe me, no man can enter the kingdom of God unless birth comes to him from water, and from the Holy Spirit* (John 3:5).

The term *to receive the Holy Spirit* is used in the Acts of the Apostles for the second stage in the sanctification of the believers. This does not mean, however, that Baptism did not involve the Holy Spirit, because Jesus said: *Believe me, no man can enter the kingdom of God unless birth comes to him from water, and from the Holy Spirit* (John 3:5). Holy Scripture does not indicate clearly at which moment Jesus actually instituted Christian Baptism, but when He Himself received baptism by the hand of John the Baptist, He showed us the *mechanism* of the sanctifying rite He intended to establish: *Jesus was baptised and, as he came straight up out of the water, suddenly heaven was opened, and he saw the Spirit of God coming down like a dove and resting upon him* (Matt. 3:16). Jesus was establishing what is called a Sacrament: an external sign that actually brings about the spiritual good it signifies. The water, habitually used for washing the body, would have, in Christian Baptism, the power to purify the soul from sin. St. Paul bears witness of it when speaking of the great love of Christ for His

Church: *He would hallow it, purify it by bathing it in the water to which his word gave life* (Eph. 5:26).

St. Peter leaves us in no doubt about the link between water and purification from sin in Baptism. *That ark which Noe was then building, in which a few souls, eight in all, found refuge as they passed through the waves, was a type of the baptism which saves us now. Our baptism is not a putting away of outward defilement; it is the test which assures us of a good conscience before God, through the Resurrection of Jesus Christ* (1 Peter 3:20-21).

Jesus had already trained His disciples in a baptismal rite similar to that of John the Baptist. St. John Apostle tells us how the Baptist's disciples complained about it: *Master, there was one with thee on the other side of the Jordan, to whom thou didst then bear testimony. We find that he is baptising now, and all are flocking to him* (John 3:26). In the next chapter John specifies: *Although it was his disciples who baptised, not Jesus himself* (John 4:2). Later on, Jesus would solemnly command them to make disciples of all nations, *baptising them in the name of the Father, and of the Son, and of the Holy Spirit* (Matt. 28:19).

Jesus' disciples must be born anew from water and the Holy Spirit; so Jesus explained to Nicodemus. *The Holy Spirit will come upon you, and you will receive strength from him* (Acts 1:8), He added before ascending into heaven. Here is the key to the understanding of the Lord's statements on the sanctifying action of the Holy Spirit. Baptism is a new birth to supernatural life; reception of the Holy Spirit is growth, strength, *power from on high* (Luke 24:49) and is now called *confirmation* because through it the

Christian is confirmed in his faith and in his adherence to the Church. Baptism makes us children of God; confirmation makes us soldiers of Christ. This explains the distinction, and yet the intimate connection, between Baptism and Confirmation: as a baby is expected to grow to full manhood, although he already possesses the dignity attached to his human condition, so the newly baptised Christian is meant to be *clothed with power from on high* (Luke 24:49) so that he *shall reach perfect manhood, that maturity which is proportioned to the completed growth of Christ* (Eph. 4:13).

Children of God

> *You are children new born, and all your craving must be for the soul's pure milk, that will nurture you into salvation once you have tasted, as you have surely tasted, the goodness of the Lord* (1 Peter 2:2-3).

Water signifies purification from sin, and this purification implies a new life in the Holy Spirit. So Baptism is the new birth Jesus spoke about to Nicodemus. When the Lord was baptised in the Jordan, as *the Holy Spirit came down upon him in bodily form, like a dove, a voice came from heaven, which said: Thou art my beloved Son, in thee I am well pleased* (Luke 3:22). Jesus Christ wanted us to participate in His divine filiation: *but all those who did welcome him, he empowered to become the children of God, all those who believe in his name; their birth came, not from human stock, not from nature's will or man's, but from God* (John 1:12-13).

When we receive baptism, we are made one with Christ. *All you who have been baptised in Christ's name have put on the person of Christ; no more Jew or Gentile, no more slave and free man, no more male and female; you are all one person in Jesus Christ* (Gal 3:27-28). Therefore we start a new life, which is a new spiritual birth: *in our baptism, we have been buried with him, died like him, that so, just as Christ was raised up by his Father's power from the dead, we too might live and move in a new kind of existence* (Rom. 6:4).

Members of the Church through Baptism

> *So all those who had taken his words to heart were baptised, and about three thousand souls were won for the Lord that day* (Acts 2:41).

The first Christians understood the teachings of Jesus as requiring the ceremony of Baptism to be admitted to the fellowship of the disciples. There are abundant references to Baptism in the Acts of the Apostles, and these refer to a baptism with water administered to the new believer to make him a disciple, a member of the Church.

The first ones to be converted through the preaching of the Apostles on Pentecost day were immediately baptised (cf. Acts 2:41). When Saul, blinded by the vision he had received from the Lord, was cured by Ananias, *he rose up, and was baptised*

(Acts 9:18). St. Paul's preaching normally concluded with the baptism of new converts: *and by now many of the Corinthians listened and found faith and were baptised* (Acts 18:8).

We know this baptism involved the use of water because in several cases it is expressly mentioned as a necessary element. When Peter saw that Cornelius and his companions had received the Holy Spirit and should therefore be admitted in the Church he exclaimed: *who will grudge us the water for baptising those men, that have received the Holy Spirit just as we did? And he gave orders that they should be baptised in the name of the Lord Jesus Christ* (Acts 10:47-48). When Philip the Deacon was preaching the word of God to the Ethiopian on the road that led to Gaza, *as they went on their way, they came to a piece of water, and the eunuch said, See, there is water here; may I not be baptised? Philip said, If thou dost believe with all thy heart, thou mayest. And he answered, I believe that Jesus Christ is the Son of God. So he had the chariot stopped, and both of them, Philip and the eunuch, went down into the water, and Philip baptised him there* (Acts 8:36-38).

Infant Baptism

> *And the Lord opened her heart, so that she was attentive to Paul's preaching. She was baptised, with all her household* (Acts 16:14-15).

Although there is no express statement in relation to the baptism of infants, one finds in the Acts of the

Apostles several indications that baptism was in fact administered to children. On various occasions, the conversion of one adult is followed by the baptism of a whole household. In Philippi, *one of those who were listening was a woman called Lydia, a purple-seller from the city of Thyatira, and a worshipper of the true God; and the Lord opened her heart, so that she was attentive to Paul's preaching. She was baptised, with all her household* (Acts 16:14-15). In those days, the fears of population explosion were non-existent and children were always received with joy as a sign of blessing from God; families were closely knit and a household without young children would seldom be found. Yet the whole household of Lydia was baptised, as was soon afterwards that of the gaoler who had asked Paul and Silas: *What am I to do to save myself? Have faith, they said to him, in the Lord Jesus; there lies salvation for thee, and for thy household. Then they preached the word of God to him, and to all that were in his house; and he, there and then, at dead of night, took them away to wash their wounds, and without delay he and his were baptised. So he led them to his home, where he put food before them, and he and all his household made rejoicing at having found faith in God* (Acts 16:30-34). When writing to the Corinthians, St. Paul recalls having baptised Crispus, Gaius and the household of Stephanas (cf. 1 Cor. 1:14-16).

In addition, we must take into account the fact that the early Christians, following St. Paul's teaching, saw in Baptism the sign of the New Covenant that was to replace the Old Covenant whose sign was circumcision. *In him you have been circumcised with a circumcision that was not man's handiwork. It was effected, not by despoiling the natural body, but by Christ's circumcision; you, by baptism, have been united with his burial, united too with his resurrection, through your faith in that exercise of power by which God raised him from the dead* (Col. 2:11-12).

Circumcision was to be administered not only to adult Jews of Abraham's generation and to proselytes, but to every new-born male child, and it is most likely that the baptismal rite soon was administered to infants, instead of circumcision, in every family of Christians converted from Judaism. True, circumcision on the eighth day had been expressly commanded by God: *Generation after generation, every male child shall be circumcised when it is eight days old* (Gen. 17:12), while no such instruction was given us by Christ. But it is interesting to observe that one of the few misdeeds that aroused Jesus' anger with his disciples was their attempt to keep children away from him: *Then they brought children to him, asking him to touch them; and his disciples rebuked those who brought them. But Jesus was indignant at seeing this: let the children come to me, he said, do not keep them back; the kingdom of God belongs to such as these. I tell you truthfully, a man who does not welcome the kingdom of God like a child will never enter into it. And so he embraced and blessed them* (Mark 10:13-16).

Circumcision was necessary to become a member of the Chosen People. *If any male person has the flesh of his foreskin uncircumcised, there is no place for him among his people; he has violated the covenant between us* (Gen. 17:14). The eight-day old Jewish baby knew nothing of God's promises to Abraham, Isaac and Jacob, and was totally unaware of his people's expectation of a Redeemer; yet he qualified to be a true member of the Chosen People. Jesus assured: *a man cannot see the kingdom of God without being born anew* (John 3:3). We also read in St. John's Gospel: *A woman in childbirth feels distress, because now her time has come; but when she has borne her child, she does not remember the distress any longer, so glad is she that a man has been born into the world* (John 16:21). The Lord calls a new-born baby a man, showing that the age makes no difference in human dignity. Why couldn't this new-born *man* receive the new birth that will make him a child of God and a member of God's Church?

Necessity of Baptism

> *He who believes and is baptised will be saved; he who refuses belief will be condemned* (Mark 16:16).

The words of the Lord as recorded by St. Mark under the inspiration of the Holy Spirit show clearly the connection between faith and baptism. The reception of baptism is the necessary consequence of the first act of faith in Jesus Christ and, right from the beginning of the life of the Church, there was no valid excuse for omitting or even postponing it – even when Cornelius and his companions had already received the Holy Spirit, and they were heard *speaking with tongues, and proclaiming the greatness of God. Then Peter said openly: who will grudge us the water for baptising these men, that have received the Holy Spirit just as we did?*

And he gave orders that they should be baptised in the name of the Lord Jesus Christ (Acts 10:46-48).

When Ananias explained to Saul what God was expecting from him, he urged him to receive Baptism without further delay. *The God of our fathers has made choice of thee to know his will, to have sight of him who is Just, and hear speech from his lips; and what thou hast seen and heard, thou shalt testify before all men. Come then, why art thou wasting time? Rise up and receive baptism, washing away thy sins at the invocation of his name* (Acts 22:14-16). One is left with the impression that Baptism is a necessary condition to receive the grace of God and to preach the word of God to others.

When Paul met in Ephesus a dozen believers who had only received John's baptism, he wasted no time preparing them for the Lord's Baptism: *So Paul told them: John baptised to bring men to repentance; but he bade the people have faith in one who was to come after him, that is, in Jesus. On hearing this, they received baptism in the name of the Lord Jesus* (Acts 19:4-5). Priscilla and Aquila must have done just the same with Apollo who *with a spirit full of zeal, used to preach and teach about the life of Jesus accurately enough, although he knew of no baptism except that of John. So he began to speak out boldly in the synagogue, whereupon Priscilla and Aquila, who had been listening, made friends with him, and explained the way of God to him more particularly* (Acts 18:25-26). No mention is made of Apollo's Baptism, but then the Acts would look more like a parish register than a History of the Early Church if they were to record the baptism of every convert. From Paul's behaviour towards the twelve men of Ephesus, we can easily infer that Apollo was baptised without any unnecessary delay.

One may object that neither the Apostles nor the 120 brethren gathered with them on Pentecost Sunday (cf. Acts 1:15) seem to have received Baptism.

First of all, one might argue that the baptism given by the Apostles (cf. John 4:1-2) when Jesus was still in their company may already have been the Life-giving Baptism that was later to be made obligatory for all when Jesus promulgated it on the day of His Ascension. No definite conclusion can be drawn from the sacred texts. But leaving aside this possibility, the fact that the Lord could have sanctified His disciples of the first hour and granted them the fullness of the Holy Spirit without previous Baptism does not excuse any of the later Christians from the obligation to fulfil the precept of receiving this Sacrament. God created Adam and Eve, but this does not exempt the rest of the human race from receiving life through the process of generation. God's power is no less now than it was at the beginning of Creation; *I tell you, God has power to raise up children to Abraham out of these very stones* (Luke 3:8), John the Baptist told the multitudes. Yet it is not part of His plan to do so.

The teachings of St. Paul in the letter to the Romans with respect to the importance of faith for man's salvation must also be understood in the context of the whole New Testament. *Thou canst find salvation if thou wilt use thy lips to confess that Jesus is the Lord, and thy heart to believe that God has raised him up from the dead. The heart has only to believe, if we are to be justified; the lips have only to make confession, if we are to be saved* (Rom. 10:9-10). These words must be read keeping in mind the intimate connection that exists between faith and baptism; *he who believes and is baptised will be saved*, the Lord had said (Mark 16:16). To St. Paul as to any Christian instructed in the Lord's teachings, it was unthinkable that a person could believe in Jesus Christ and yet neglect to fulfil the Lord's command of receiving Baptism. However, if such a person remained unbaptised out of ignorance or material impossibility, his faith would be sufficient to save him (which is what we now call baptism of desire).

4

The Sanctifying Action of the Holy Spirit: II – Soldiers of Christ

The fullness of the Holy Spirit, power from on high

> *And behold I am sending down upon you the gift promised by my Father; you must wait in the city until you are clothed with power from on high* (Luke 24:49).

During the Last Supper, Jesus had promised a Gift from His Father to those who would be faithful to His teachings: *If you have any love for me, you must keep the commandments which I give you; and then I will ask the Father, and he will give you another to befriend you, one who is to dwell continually with you for ever. It is the truth-giving Spirit, for whom the world can find no room, because it cannot see him, cannot recognise him; he will be continually at your side, nay, he will be in you* (John 14:15-17).

The Holy Spirit will give knowledge, wisdom and fortitude to profess the Faith even in times of adversity. Christians will suffer persecutions at the hands of men, but they must put all their trust in the Holy Spirit who will assist them: *words will be given you when the time comes; it is not you who speak, it is the Spirit of your Father that speaks in you. Brothers will be given up to execution by their brothers, and children by their fathers; children will rise up against their parents and will compass their deaths, and you will be hated by all men because you bear my name; that man will be saved, who endures to the last* (Matt. 10:19-22).

On the day of His Ascension, Jesus reminded the Apostles of this promise: *and behold, I am sending down upon you the gift which was promised by my Father; you must wait in the city until you are clothed with power from on high* (Luke 24:49). This aspect of power, of strength, is most emphasised in the Acts of the Apostles. When the earthly-minded apostles ask Him whether He will finally restore Israel's dominion, He directs their thoughts to more supernatural considerations: *Enough for you, that the Holy Spirit will come upon you, and you will receive strength from him* (Acts 1:8).

Before the Holy Spirit had come down upon them, the Apostles were fearful, they lacked daring. St. John tells us how, after the arrest and crucifixion of Jesus, they carefully locked themselves in the room where they stayed: *for fear of the Jews, the disciples had locked the doors of the room in which they had assembled* (John 20:19). Even after they had seen the Risen Lord, they were still afraid: *so eight days afterwards, once more the disciples were within, and Thomas was with them; and the doors were locked* (John 20:26).

But on Pentecost Sunday, *all at once a sound came from heaven like that of a strong wind blowing, and filled the whole house where they were sitting. Then appeared to them what seemed to be tongues of fire, which parted and came to rest on each of them; and they were all filled with the Holy Spirit, and began to speak in strange languages, as the Spirit gave utterance to each* (Acts 2:2-4). The noise attracted a crowd of people, and this time the Apostles were no longer filled with fear; they spoke with assurance, proclaiming the Good News of the Lord Jesus. Some time later Peter, who had been afraid of a maid-servant when his Master was arrested, was able to face the rulers and scribes of Jerusalem who had gathered to question him. *Then Peter was filled with the Holy Spirit and said to them: Rulers of the people, elders of Israel, listen to me* (Acts 4:8). On his return, the Christian community prayed for God's help and *when they had finished praying, the place in which they had gathered rocked to and fro, and they were all filled with the Holy Spirit, and began to preach the word of God with confidence* (Acts 4:31).

Stephen the Deacon is a good example of the strength given by the Holy Spirit. So filled was he with the Holy Spirit that God worked miracles through him. *And Stephen, full of grace and power, performed great miracles and signs among the people* (Acts 6:8). He was able to explain the Faith and defend it against any attack: many came forward to debate with him, *but they were no match for Stephen's wisdom, and for the Spirit which then gave utterance* (Acts 6:10). In front of his accusers, he made the profession of faith that led to his death: *but he, full of the Holy Spirit, fastened his eyes on heaven, and saw here the glory of God, and Jesus standing at God's right hand; I see heaven opening, he said, and the Son of Man standing at the right hand of*

God (Acts 7:55).

To receive the fullness of the Holy Spirit, it was necessary to have received Baptism. When Peter had preached for the first time on Pentecost Sunday, the people were anxious to find salvation: *and they asked Peter and his fellow apostles, Brethren, what must we do? Repent, Peter said to them, and be baptised, everyone of you, in the name of Jesus Christ, to have your sins forgiven; then you will receive the gift of the Holy Spirit* (Acts 2:37-38).

Receiving the Holy Spirit: The Sacrament of Confirmation

> *Then the Apostles began to lay their hands on them, so that the Holy Spirit was given them* (Acts 8:17).

The Bible shows how the Holy Spirit was received through a rite that had all the characteristics of what we call a Sacrament: a minister performed upon a subject an external action that actually achieved the spiritual effect it represented. To lay one's hand upon a person is in the Bible a sign of blessing; Jesus laid his hands upon children and blessed them (cf. Mark 10:16). With this sign of blessing, the Source of all grace descended upon the disciples. We have already seen how the direct intervention of the Holy Spirit upon the first disciples on Pentecost Sunday and upon Cornelius and his companions was the exception rather than the rule. Very soon, it appeared that the Holy

Spirit was granted only through the ministry of one of the Apostles, with the performance of a specific rite: the laying on of hands.

When the first persecution scattered Christians all over Judaea and Samaria, Philip the Deacon preached Christ in Samaria. There, Simon the Magician was converted along with many of his compatriots. They were baptised, but did not receive the fullness of the Holy Spirit until Peter and John came and *prayed for them, that they might receive the Holy Spirit, who had not, as yet, come down on any of them; they had received nothing so far except baptism in the name of the Lord Jesus. Then the apostles began to lay their hands on them, so that the Holy Spirit was given them* (Acts 8:15-17). The direct connection between the imposition of the Apostles' hands and the reception of the Holy Spirit is made evident by the attitude of Simon who saw in it some sort of magic power that he wished to master. *Simon, seeing that the Holy Spirit was granted through the imposition of the apostles' hands, offered them money; Let me too, he said, have such powers that when I lay my hands on anyone he will receive the Holy Spirit* (Acts 8:18-19).

So Philip did not possess this power of conferring the Holy Spirit. He was only a deacon, not a bishop. Peter and John had to come to confirm the Samaritans.

Years later, St. Paul went to Ephesus and found some disciples there. He asked them whether they had received the Holy Spirit since they learned to believe; this question shows that not every man who was converted to Christ automatically received the fullness of the Holy Spirit. Anyone could baptise, but only the Apostles and their successors the Bishops could confirm.* It appeared that those disciples had only received John's baptism. So after instructing them about Jesus Christ, Paul had those men baptised, and then he laid his hands upon them. It was not the acceptance of Christ as their Saviour that made the Holy Spirit come upon them, though of course it was a necessary pre-requisite; neither was it Baptism alone, but the imposition of the hands of the Apostle Paul: *and when Paul laid his hands upon them, the Holy Spirit came down on them, and they spoke with tongues, and prophesied* (Acts 19:6).

The Holy Spirit, the gift of the Father

The spirit you have now received is not, as of old, a spirit of slavery, to govern you by fear; it is the spirit of adoption, which makes us cry out, Abba, Father. The Spirit himself thus assures our spirit, that we are children of God; and if we are his children, then we are his heirs too; heirs of God, sharing the inheritance of Christ; only we must share his sufferings, if we

---

* However, the power to confirm can be, and in fact often is, delegated by Bishops to simple priests, as authorised by the Pope. This extraordinary power to confirm is a constituent part of the power of consecration received by the priest in Holy Orders, but it is limited and can be used only in virtue of the papal power of the Keys.

are to share his glory (Rom. 8:15-17).

A person who reads the Acts of the Apostles and the Letters of St. Paul without seeking the guidance of the Church can easily get the impression that the gifts of the Holy Spirit consist principally in extraordinary supernatural manifestations such as those that took place on Pentecost Sunday. Yet St. Paul, in his First Letter to the Corinthians, makes it clear that the gifts of tongues, of prophecy, of healing etc. are not granted to everyone. *Are all of us apostles? all prophets, all teachers? Have all miraculous powers, or gifts of healing? Can all speak with tongues, can all interpret? Prize the best gifts of heaven. Meanwhile, I can show you a way which is better than any other* (1 Cor. 12:29-31); and he goes on praising the greatest gift of all, the only one truly necessary because if we have this gift, then we lack nothing: charity, love of God. *The time will come when we shall outgrow prophecy, when speaking with tongues will come to an end, when knowledge will be swept away; we shall never have finished with charity. Our knowledge, our prophecy, are only glimpses of the truth; and these glimpses will be swept away when the time of fulfilment comes* (1 Cor. 13:8-10). And he concludes: *meanwhile, faith, hope and charity persist, all three; but the greatest of them all is charity* (1 Cor. 13:13).

Already in Baptism we had received the gifts of Faith, Hope and Charity through the action of the Holy Spirit. When we receive the fullness of the Holy Spirit our Faith, Hope and Charity (Love of God) are strengthened. Faith: *in him you too learned to believe, and had the seal set on your faith by the promised gift of* the Holy Spirit (Eph. 1:13). Hope: *May God, the author of our hope, fill you with all joy and peace in your believing; so that you may have hope in abundance, through the power of the Holy Spirit* (Rom. 15:13). Charity: *The love of God has been poured out in our hearts by the Holy Spirit, whom we have received* (Rom. 5:5). The principal effect of the in-dwelling of the Holy Spirit cannot be a variety of gifts that are not received by all Christians and that are not to last within us after we undergo bodily death. When adopting us as His own children, God the Father granted us the Spirit of His Son. *To prove that you are sons, God has sent out the Spirit of His Son into your hearts, crying out in us, Abba, Father* (Gal. 4:6). This divine filiation will continue in Heaven, where it will reach its full meaning, as God has created us for this very purpose, He *who has blessed us, in Christ, with every spiritual blessing, higher than heaven itself. He has chosen us out, in Christ, before the foundation of the world, to be saints, to be blameless in his sight, for love of him; marking us out beforehand (so his will decreed) to be his adopted children through Jesus Christ* (Eph. 1:3-5). Indeed, *a man cannot belong to Christ unless he has the Spirit of Christ* (Rom. 8:9).

What are the effects of this in-dwelling of the Spirit of Jesus Christ granted to us by God? Through the prophet Isaias, God revealed the characteristics of the spirit of the Lord that was to rest upon the Redeemer: *From the stock of Jesse a scion shall burgeon yet; out of his roots a flower shall spring. One shall be born, on whom the spirit of the Lord will rest; a spirit wise and discerning, a spirit prudent and strong, a spirit of knowledge and of piety, and ever fear of the Lord shall fill his heart* (Isaias 11:1-2). The Old Testament does not contain any express revelation of the Mystery of the Holy Trinity (three Persons in one God), but in this passage of Scripture Christian Tradition has always recognised the existence of Seven Gifts of the Holy Spirit, inseparable from the presence of the Holy Spirit Himself in the soul of a Christian: wisdom and understanding, prudence and fortitude, knowledge, piety and fear of the Lord. These gifts are granted to all who receive the Holy Spirit, and they are intended to last for ever, though in a more perfect way once we reach everlasting life: in heaven no-one will prophesy any more, nor speak with tongues, but we shall all have perfect knowledge and love of divine things (Wisdom), a most deep understanding of supernatural mysteries (Understanding), we shall know what it is right to do (Prudence) and no weakness shall prevent us from doing it (Fortitude), we shall have evidence of the relative value of created goods (Knowledge), we shall love God with the purest love (Piety) and render Him the honour due to His Infinite Majesty (Fear of the Lord).

This is the Spirit of Jesus Christ sent into our hearts by God. This Gift is not evident in every Christian upon whom the Apostles' or the Bishops' hands were laid, and yet God's promise cannot fail. What happens to some Christians is that they do not make use of God's Gift, they do not make the necessary effort to make it bear fruit. We can say that they have locked God's Gift away and have forgotten about it; the Gift is there, in their possession, but is rendered ineffective by their lack of cooperation with God's grace. It is the parable of the pounds: *There was a man of noble birth, who went away to a distant*

*country, to have the royal title bestowed on him, and so
return. And he summoned ten of his servants, to whom
he gave ten pounds, and said to them: Trade with this
while I am away. But his fellow citizens hated him, and
sent ambassadors after him to say, We will not have this
man for our king. Afterwards, when he came back as
king, he sent forth for the servants to whom he had
entrusted the money, to find out how much each of them
had gained by his use of it* (Luke 19:12-15). We must
make use of God's highest Gift if we do not wish to
hear His words of condemnation. But no-one can deny
the fact that we have received the Holy Spirit when we
were confirmed and heard from the lips of an Apostle's
successor: *Receive the Holy Spirit, the Gift of the Father.*

Other spiritual gifts

> *Since you have set your hearts on spiritual
> gifts, ask for them in abundant measure,
> but only so as to strengthen the faith of
> the church* (1 Cor. 14:12).

In his First Letter to the Corinthians, St. Paul
speaks of the variety of spiritual gifts granted by the
Holy Spirit. *And yet there are different kinds of gifts,
though it is the same Spirit who gives them, just as there
are different kinds of service, though it is the same Lord
we serve, and different manifestations of power, though it
is the same who manifests his power everywhere in all of
us. The revelation of the Spirit is imparted to each, to
make the best advantage of it. One learns to speak with
wisdom, by the power of the Spirit, another to speak with*

knowledge, with the same Spirit for his rule; one, through the same Spirit, is given faith; another, through the same Spirit, powers of healing; one can perform miracles, one can prophesy, another can test the spirit of the prophets; one can speak in different tongues, another can interpret the tongues; but all this is the work of one and the same Spirit, who distributes his gifts as he will to each severally (1 Cor. 12:4-11). As the various members of the body contribute, each in its own way, to the welfare of the whole body, so, St. Paul explains, *you are Christ's body, organs of it depending upon each other. God has given us different positions in the Church, apostles first, then prophets, and thirdly teachers; then come miraculous powers, then gifts of healing, works of mercy, the management of affairs, speaking with different tongues, and interpreting prophecy* (1 Cor. 12:27-30).

But those gifts are meant for the good of others, for the growth of the Church, for the instruction and strengthening of the faith of others. They do not imply necessarily a state of holiness in the person who receives those gifts. After all, most of the Prophets of the Old Testament, inspired by the Holy Spirit, were men of faith; but we read in Holy Scripture that Caiphas prophesied when he advised the council of chief priests and Pharisees: *You have no perception at all; you do not reflect that it is best for us if one man is put to death for the sake of the people, to save a whole nation from destruction. It was not of his own impulse that he said this; holding the high priesthood as he did in that year, he was able to prophesy that Jesus was to die for the sake of the nation; and not only for that nation's sake, but so as to bring together into one all God's children, scattered far and wide* (John 11:49-52). So the

Bible testifies that the Holy Spirit sometimes chooses
to entrust His messages to an undeserving person.

Those *external* spiritual gifts are useful only if they
serve their purpose, which is the sanctification of
others. St. Paul speaks very strongly about this, and let
us not forget that the Holy Spirit is the one speaking
through the inspired writer. The gift of prophecy ranks
much higher than the gift of tongues, because *the
prophet speaks to edify, to encourage, to comfort his
fellow men. By talking a strange tongue a man may
strengthen his own spirit; by prophesying he can
strengthen the faith of the Church. I would gladly see you
all speaking with strange tongues, but I would rather you
should prophesy, because the prophet ranks higher than
the man who speaks with strange tongues. It would be
different if he could translate them, to strengthen the faith
of the Church; but as things are, brethren, what good can
I do you by coming and talking to you in strange
languages, instead of addressing you with a revelation, or
a manifestation of inner knowledge, or a prophecy, or
words of instruction?* (1 Cor. 14:3-6) And the Apostle
concludes: *Since you have set your hearts on spiritual
gifts, ask for them in abundant measure, but only so as to
strengthen the faith of the church; the man who can
speak in a strange tongue should pray for the power to
interpret it* (1 Cor. 14:12-13). St. Paul insists on the fact
that speaking in strange tongues unintelligible to others
is not a gift to covet and to show off: *If I use a strange
tongue when I offer prayer, my spirit is praying, but my
mind reaps no advantage from it. What, then, is my drift?
Why, I mean to use mind as well as spirit when I offer
prayer, use mind as well as spirit when I sing psalms. If
thou dost pronounce a blessing in this spiritual fashion,*

how can one who takes his place among the uninstructed say Amen to thy thanksgiving? He cannot tell what thou art saying. Thou, true enough, art duly giving thanks, but the other's faith is not strengthened. Thank God, I can speak any of the tongues you use; but in the church I would rather speak five words which my mind utters, for your instruction, than ten thousand in a strange tongue (1 Cor. 14:14-19).

Those gifts were not normally compelling, irresistible motions of the Holy Spirit. They did not produce a trance, a state of ecstasy. Sometimes indeed there were abuses, with some people letting themselves be carried away by their emotions, and speaking all at once without paying any attention to their companions. Such an attitude is sternly reproved by St. Paul. *And now what will happen if the uninstructed or the unbeliever come in when the whole church has met together, and find everyone speaking with strange tongues at once? Will they not say you are mad?* (1 Cor. 14:23). In the case of the gift of prophecy, less harm can be done by excessive enthusiasm: *whereas, if some unbeliever or some uninstructed person comes in when all alike are prophesying, everyone will read his thoughts, everyone will scrutinise him, all that is kept hidden in his heart will be revealed; and so he will fall on his face and worship God, publicly confessing that God is indeed among you* (1 Cor. 14:24-25).

However St. Paul, inspired by the Holy Spirit, calls upon Christians to control themselves, which means that there was no irresistible impulse coming from above. *What am I urging, then, brethren? Why, when you meet together, each of you with a psalm to sing, or some doctrine to impart, or a revelation to give, or ready to speak in strange tongues, or to interpret them, see that all is done to your spiritual advantage. If there is speaking with strange tongues, do not let more than two speak, or three at the most; let each take his turn, with someone to interpret for him, and if he can find nobody to interpret, let him be silent in the church, conversing with his own spirit and with God. As for the prophets, let two or three of them speak, while the rest sit in judgement on their prophecies. If some revelation comes to another who is sitting by, let him who spoke first keep silence; there is room for you all to prophesy one by one, so that the whole company may receive instruction and comfort; and it is for the prophets to exercise control over their own spiritual gifts* (1 Cor. 14:26-32).

The gift of tongues

> *So, when the noise of this went abroad, the crowd which gathered was in bewilderment; each man severally heard them speak in his own language. And they were all beside themselves with astonishment. Are they not all Galilean speaking? they asked. How is it that each of us hears them talking his own native tongue?* (Acts 2:6-8)

Nowadays most people tend to think that the gift of tongues consists in pronouncing, under a strong motion of the Holy Spirit, unintelligible words that God alone understands. Let us see what the Bible says.

The very first manifestation of the gift of tongues

took place on Pentecost Sunday, when the Holy Spirit
came down upon the Apostles in all His power. As a
result, they were able to proclaim the wonders of God
in foreign languages they had never learned before, so
that their hearers coming from far-away lands could
hear the Good News in their own native tongue. It is
worth reading carefully what the Acts tell us about it,
noting the insistence with which the inspired writer
describes the surprise of the people at hearing a group
of Galileans speaking in many different languages: *And
they were all filled with the Holy Spirit and began to
speak in strange languages, as the Spirit gave utterance to
each. Among those who were dwelling in Jerusalem at
this time were devout Jews from every country under
heaven; so, when the noise of this went abroad, the
crowd which gathered was in bewilderment; each man
severally heard them speak in his own language. And
they were all beside themselves with astonishment. Are
they not all Galilean speaking? they asked. How is it that
each of us hears them talking his own native tongue?
There are Parthians among us, and Medes, and
Elamites; our homes are in Mesopotamia, or Judaea, or
Cappadocia; in Pontus or Asia, Phrygia or Pamphylia,
Egypt or the parts of Lybia round Cyrene; some of us are
Jews and others proselytes; there are Cretans among us
too, and Arabians; and each has been hearing them tell
of God's wonders in his own language. So they were all
beside themselves with perplexity, and asked one
another, What can this mean?* (Acts 2:4-12).

   The tongues spoken by many of the first
Christians were not mystical languages, but simply
foreign languages: *How can it be known what your
message is, if you speak in a language whose accents*

cannot be understood? Your words will fall on empty air. No doubt all these different languages exist somewhere in the world, and each of them has its significance; but if I cannot understand what the language means, the effect is that I am a foreigner to the man who is speaking, and he is a foreigner to me (1 Cor. 14:9-11). St. Paul himself knew all those languages: *Thank God, I can speak any of the tongues you use* (1 Cor. 14:18). But he used those languages only when they were needed, i.e. to transmit the Good News of Jesus Christ to foreigners.

The Apostles had to spread the Gospel throughout the world. According to an ancient tradition, Thomas travelled as far as India and St. James converted Spain; without a special gift from God, it would have been practically impossible to communicate with the local people and teach them the truths revealed by Christ. The capacity to speak strange tongues (i.e. foreign languages) was necessary for the first expansion of Christianity. It appears, however, that some did not use it only for this purpose but also for praising God among their fellow citizens, and this motivated St. Paul's rebuke to the Corinthians: to speak in an unknown language to an assembly of Greek speaking Corinthians was as pointless as delivering a Sunday Sermon to a Nigerian congregation in Chinese or in Swahili. Sometimes the person speaking in a strange tongue did not himself understand what he was saying, while another person received the gift of understanding and translating what was said. In those cases, however, St. Paul's command is clear and straightforward: *the man who can speak in a strange tongue should pray for the power to interpret it* (1 Cor. 14:13), without which he may speak only in the presence of an interpreter, *and if he can find nobody to interpret, let him be silent in the church, conversing with his own spirit and with God* (1 Cor. 14:28).

Nowadays, the Church has spread all over the world. Christianity is firmly established in most countries, and people can learn about Christ through their own countrymen. With the development and generalisation of formal schooling, the learning of foreign languages is much more accessible than it ever was before. For these reasons God, who prefers to act in ordinary ways, does not grant the gift of tongues so abundantly in the same way as He did in apostolic times. *The time will come*, St. Paul said, *when speaking with tongues will come to an end* (1 Cor. 13:8).

Nowadays the Holy Spirit, without any extraordinary manifestations and without dispensing men from the laborious study of foreign languages, grants the gift of tongues to all those who *hunger and thirst for holiness* (cf. Matt. 5:6) and wish to be *fishers of men* (cf. Luke 5:10): the capacity to make themselves understood, to adapt themselves to their hearer's mentality to find the most effective way to communicate their faith and their knowledge of God. Such gift of tongues has been present in the Church throughout all centuries and permitted the growth of the Church in the five continents.

The gifts of prophecy and of teaching

> *Make charity your aim, the spiritual gifts your aspiration; and, by preference, the gift of prophecy* (1 Cor. 14:1).

People keen on extraordinary manifestations of the Holy Spirit attach great importance to the gift of tongues, and not as much to the gift of prophecy so strongly recommended by the Holy Spirit Himself through the mouth of St. Paul. The gift of prophecy seems very related to that of teaching, although there is a distinction: *God has given us different positions in the church; apostles first, then prophets and thirdly teachers* (1 Cor. 12:38). The gift of prophecy enabled a Christian to know the secrets of the heart, to read the thoughts of others (cf. 1 Cor. 14:24-25) as well as to express God's mysteries (cf. 1 Cor. 14:30-31). The gift of teaching simply made a Christian particularly apt to impart to others his knowledge of Christ's teachings. Every Christian community had its bishops, its prophets and its teachers, as was the case in Antioch: *the Church at Antioch had as its prophets and teachers Barnabas, and Simon who was called Niger, and Lucius of Cyrene, and Manahen, foster-brother of Herod the Tetrarch, and Saul* (Acts 13:1).

Here again, there is no indication that such gifts were always surrounded with extraordinary manifestations of power from Heaven, or that prophets and teachers spoke in a state of trance. They had the grace of God to instruct others, to communicate to them what God had put in their own hearts. *A good man utters what is good from his heart's store of goodness* (Luke 6:45).

According to the Acts of the Apostles, the task of prophets was to encourage Christians and strengthen their faith. *So they took their leave and went down to Antioch, where they called the multitude together and delivered the letter to them; and they, upon reading it, were rejoiced at this encouragement. Judas and Silas, for they were prophets too, said much to encourage the brethren and establish their faith; they stayed there for some time before the brethren let them go home, in peace, to those who had sent them* (Acts 15:30-33).

Sometimes prophets would receive special revelations from God, as it used to happen to the prophets of the Old Testament. *At this time some prophets from Jerusalem visited Antioch; and one of these, Agabus by name, stood up and prophesied through the Spirit that a great famine was to come upon the whole world, as it did in the reign of the emperor Claudius* (Acts 11:27-28). This same Agabus, years later, had another message for Paul in Caesarea: *During our stay of several days there, a prophet named Agabus came down from Judaea. When he visited us, he took up Paul's girdle, and bound his own hands and feet with it; then he said: thus speaks the Holy Spirit, The man to whom this girdle belongs will be bound, like this, by the Jews at Jerusalem, and given over into the hands of the Gentiles* (Acts 21:10-11). Ananias acted as a prophet when he carried God's message to Saul (cf. Acts 9:10-18). So did Philip when God sent him to convert the Ethiopian (cf. Acts 8:26-40). Yet prophecy must have taken place in a very natural way as St. Paul tells us there was no obvious sign of its authenticity. There must have been abuses very early in the life of the Church, as the Bible warns us of the need to discern between true and false prophecy. *As for the prophets, let two or three of them speak, while the rest sit in judgement on their prophecies* (1 Cor. 14:29). St. Paul recommended: *Do not stifle the utterances of the Spirit, do not hold prophecy in low esteem; and yet you must scrutinise it all carefully, retaining only what is good, and rejecting all that has a look of evil about it* (1 Thess. 5:20-22). St. Peter warned Christians about false prophets: *There were false prophets, too, among God's people. So, among you, there will be false teachers, covertly introducing pernicious ways of thoughts, and denying the Master who redeemed them, to their own speedy undoing* (2 Peter 2:1). So did St. John: *Not all prophetic spirits, brethren, deserve your credence; you must put them to the test, to see whether they come from God. Many false prophets have made their appearance in the world. This is the test by which God's spirit is to be recognised; every spirit which acknowledges Jesus Christ as having come to us in human flesh has God for its author; and no spirit which would disunite Jesus comes from God* (1 John 4:1-3).

To acknowledge Jesus Christ is not only to say, 'I believe in Him.' *The kingdom of heaven will not give entrance to every man who calls me Master, Master; only to the man that does the will of my Father who is in heaven. There are many who will say to me, when that day comes, Master, Master, was it not in thy name we prophesied? Was it not in thy name that we performed many miracles? Whereupon I will tell them openly, You were never friends of mine; depart from me, you that traffic in wrong-doing* (Matt. 7:21-23). Jesus had reproached the Jews: *How is it that you call me, Master, Master, and will not do what I bid you?* (Luke 6:46). He told those whom he sent to preach: *He who listens to you listens to me; he who despises you despises me; and he who despises me, despises him that sent me* (Luke 10:16) and He entrusted to Peter the keys, i.e. the supreme authority, in His Church.

He commanded us to obey Peter when He entrusted to him the keys of the kingdom of Heaven (cf. Matt. 16:19) and to obey the Bishops when He sent His Apostles to *go out, making disciples of all nations, and baptising them in the name of the Father, and of the Son, and of the Holy Spirit, teaching them to observe all the commandments which I have given you. And behold I am with you all through the days that are coming, until the consummation of the world* (Matt. 28:19-21).

So the test of true prophecy is conformity to the traditional teaching of the Church and submission to the lawful authorities in the Church.

The gifts of prophecy and of teaching are found in abundance all throughout the history of the Church and were manifested in the lives of many saints, some of them Popes, like St. Gregory the Great, Bishops such as St. Ambrose and St. Francis de Sales, others simple priests such as the holy Curé of Ars, or religious full of missionary zeal like St. Francis Xavier. They are found in the lives of saintly women who certainly never preached in the churches, but devoted their lives to teaching (e.g. St. Angela of Merici) or received messages from Heaven which they faithfully transmitted to the lawful authorities (e.g. St. Joan of Arc, St. Catherine of Siena and St. Bernadette). They are also found in varying degrees in the lives of all ordinary Christians who strive to be holy and to bring the light of faith to their friends and colleagues.

Miraculous powers, gifts of healing

Where believers go, these signs shall go

with them; they will cast out devils in my
name, they will speak in tongues that are
strange to them; they will take up serpents
in their hands, and drink poisonous
draughts without harm; they will lay their
hands upon the sick and make them
recover (Mark 16:17-18).

We read in the Acts of the Apostles how Christ's
promise of extraordinary signs became a reality in the
life of the early Christians. To go through all the
miracles told by St. Luke would be a long task. It is
enough for our purpose to quote one passage related to
the miracles worked by God's power through Peter:
They even used to bring sick folk into the streets, and lay
them down there on beds and pallets, in the hope that
even the shadow of Peter, as he passed by, might fall
upon one of them here and there, and so they would be
healed of their infirmities. From neighbouring cities, too,
the common people flocked to Jerusalem, bringing with
them the sick and those who were troubled by unclean
spirits; and all of them were cured (Acts 5:15-16).

The Bible shows us Paul casting out devils (cf.
Acts 16:16-18), curing the sick (cf. Acts 14:7-9), raising
the dead (cf. Acts 20:8-12), and remaining unharmed
by the bite of a viper (cf. Acts 28:3-6).

These miraculous gifts have always been present
in the Church as the lives of countless saints bear
witness to it. Nowadays there are miraculous cures
obtained by ardent prayer and trust in God. But, more
important than any material miracle are the spiritual
miracles that take place day after day in the lives of
Christians who know they are called by God, through

the grace of their Baptism, to work to extend the Kingdom of God on earth.

Pope St. Gregory the Great (540-604) explained how Jesus Christ's promises were made a reality in the daily life of Christians: *Christians free men from serpents, when they uproot evil from their hearts by exhorting them to do good... They lay their hands on the sick and cure them, when they see their neighbour flagging in his good work and they offer to help in so many ways, strengthening him with their example. These miracles are all the greater in that they are worked in spiritual things and give life not to bodies but to souls. You too, if you do not weaken, will be able to work these wonders, with the help of God* (Homiliae in Evangelia, 29:4;PL 76, 1215-1216). And in contemporary times the Venerable Josemaría Escrivá echoes the words of the great Father of the Church: *If we struggle daily to become saints, each of us in his own situation in the world and through his own job or profession, in our ordinary lives, then I assure you that God will make us into instruments that can work miracles and, if necessary, miracles of the most extraordinary kind. We will give sight to the blind. Who could not relate thousands of cases of people, blind almost from the day they were born, recovering their sight and receiving all the splendour of Christ's light? And others who were deaf, or dumb, who could not hear or pronounce words fitting to God's children ... Their senses have been purified and now they listen and speak as men, not animals. 'In nomine Iesu!' In the name of Jesus his Apostles enable the cripple to move and walk, when previously he had been incapable of doing anything useful; and that other lazy character, who knew his duties but didn't fulfil them... In the Lord's name, 'surge et ambula', rise up and walk.*

Another man was dead, rotting, smelling like a corpse: he hears God's voice, as in the miracle of the son of the widow at Naim: 'Young man, I say to you, rise up.' We will work miracles like Christ did, like the first apostles did. Maybe you yourself, and I, have benefited from such wonders. Perhaps we were blind, or deaf, or paralysed; perhaps we had the stench of death, and the word of Our Lord has lifted us up from our abject state. If we love Christ, if we follow him sincerely, if we stop seeking ourselves and seek him alone, then in his name we will be able to give to others, freely, what we have freely received (Friends of God, 262).

Works of mercy and the management of affairs

> *Then come miraculous powers, then gifts of healing, works of mercy, the management of affairs, speaking with different tongues, and interpreting prophecy* (1 Cor. 12:28).

Two of the gifts granted by the Holy Spirit for the benefit of the Church are usually forgotten by those who give the highest importance to extraordinary manifestations of the in-dwelling of the Holy Spirit in the Christian's soul. Yet works of mercy and the management of affairs, according to St. Paul, rank higher than the gift of tongues.

Both gifts are somehow related. The first one moves a person to perform acts of charity towards others, seeing in them Christ Himself. *Come, you that have received a blessing from my Father, take possession of the kingdom which has been prepared for you since the foundation of the world. For I was hungry, and you gave me food, thirsty and you gave me drink; I was a stranger, and you brought me home, naked, and you clothed me, sick, and you cared for me, a prisoner, and you came to me* (Matt. 25:34-36), because *when you did it to one of the least of my brethren here, you did it to me* (Matt. 25:40).

In addition to those seven corporal works of mercy, the Church acknowledges seven spiritual ones: to admonish the sinner, to instruct the ignorant, to counsel the doubtful, to comfort the sorrowful, to bear wrongs patiently, to forgive injuries, to pray for the living and for the dead. St. Paul was making reference to them when he wrote to the Thessalonians: *And, brethren, let us make this appeal to you: warn the vagabonds, encourage the faint-hearted, support the waverers, be patient towards all. See to it that nobody repays injury with injury* (1 Thess. 5:14-15).

From the very beginning of the life of the Church, Christians cared for the sick, the poor, the afflicted, and all people in need of spiritual or material help. First, the Apostles themselves were the ones organising the works of mercy. Among the believers of the first hour, *none of them was destitute; all those who owned farms or houses used to sell them, and bring the price of what they had sold to lay it at the Apostles' feet, so that each could have what share of it he needed* (Acts 4:34-35). This behaviour was not a compulsory requirement of the Church, but a free act of generosity; indeed when Peter reproached Ananias for having lied about the price of the estate he had sold, he told him: *Unsold, the property was thine; after the sale, the money was at thy disposal; what has put it into your heart so to act? It is God, not man, thou hast defrauded* (Acts 5:4).

So what can be called *the property* or *the riches* of the Church were used for the benefit of the Christian people, for the relief of the poor. Soon, it was felt that the administration of works of mercy needed more attention than the Apostles could give, and so it was decided to appoint deacons for that purpose. *It is too much that we should have to forgo preaching God's word, and bestow our care upon tables. Come then, brethren, you must find among you seven men who are well spoken of, full of the Holy Spirit and of wisdom, for us to put in charge of this business* (Acts 6:2-3). The deacons were the first ones upon whom the gift of management of affairs was bestowed: they were in charge of administering the Church's property (essentially donations received), which would be used for three purposes: the dignity of public worship, the sober, but worthy sustenance of those who dedicated their lives to the Gospel, and the performance of works of mercy.

It would be against the spirit of the Gospel to celebrate public acts of divine worship at the smallest possible cost while dedicating all the resources of the Church to alms-giving. It would mean leaving the worst for God, as Cain did. Jesus was born in the most absolute poverty, He lived a humble life as a carpenter's son in Nazareth, and during His public life, He had nowhere to lay His head (cf. Luke 9:58). Yet He was very well dressed, with a cloak which was without seam, woven from the top throughout, most probably made or bought for Him by His mother, sufficiently valuable for the soldiers to be keenly interested in owning it: *so they said to one another, Better not to tear it; let us cast lots to decide whose it shall be* (John 19:24). In His journeys, He benefited from the generosity of the holy women *who ministered to him with the means they had* (Luke 8:3). The Apostles practised alms-giving frequently; when Jesus sent Judas out of the Cenacle, *some of them thought, since Judas kept the common purse, that Jesus was saying to him, Go and buy what we need for the feast, or bidding him give some alms to the poor* (John 13:29). Jesus recommended total poverty to the rich young man: *If thou hast a mind to be perfect, go home and sell all that belongs to thee; give it to the poor, and so the treasure thou hast shall be in heaven; then come back and follow me* (Matt. 19:21). Yet, when Mary of Bethany poured a pound of pure spikenard ointment over Jesus' feet, arousing Judas' indignation, Jesus defended her action. Judas was arguing: *Why should not this ointment have been sold? It would have fetched three hundred silver pieces, and alms might have been given to the poor* (John 12:5). But Jesus declared: *Why do you vex the woman? She did well to treat me so* (Matt. 26:10). It is a duty of faith and love to be as magnificent as possible in all the things related to divine worship.

Donations received by the Church are also destined to ensure the sustenance of the clergy. Jesus had clearly stated the principle that *the labourer has a right to his maintenance* (Matt. 10:10). And St. Paul reaffirmed it: *Your teachers are to have a share in all that their disciples have to bestow. Make no mistake about it; you cannot cheat God* (Gal. 6:6-7).

The administration of the affairs of the Church requires a true gift from God. *The spiritual gifts we have differ, according to the special grace which has been assigned to each. If a man is a prophet, let him prophesy as far as the measure of his faith will let him. The administrator must be content with his administration, the teacher, with his work of teaching, the preacher, with his preaching. Each must perform his own task well; giving alms with generosity, exercising authority with anxious care, or doing works of mercy smilingly* (Rom. 12:6-8).

It is a gift, because it requires more than just a good business sense to be able to yield spiritual dividends. Speaking of the organisation of the collection for the relief of the Christians of Judaea, St. Paul explains: *The administration, remember, of this public service does more than supply the needs of the saints; it yields, besides, a rich harvest of thanksgiving in the name of the Lord. This administration makes men praise God for the spirit of obedience which you show in confessing the gospel of Christ, and the generosity which you show in sharing your goods with these and with all men; and they will intercede, too, on your behalf as the abundant measure of grace which God bestows on you warms their hearts towards you* (2 Cor. 9:12-14).

St. Lawrence was a deacon in charge of the distribution of alms to the poor. He was arrested by the pagans who tortured him to make him reveal the hiding place of the treasures of the Church. He pointed at a group of poor people and exclaimed: *these are the treasure of the Church*. In the sixteenth century, at a time when Calvin separated himself from the Church and taught that the elect were blessed by God with material goods in this world, and sinners punished with poverty and illness, the true Church, faithful to her Christian vocation and receptive to the gifts of the Holy Spirit, continued steadfastly performing works of mercy, recognising Christ in the poor, the sick and the afflicted.

The gift that really matters

Prize the best gifts of heaven. Meanwhile, I can show you a way which is better than any other. I may speak with every tongue that men and angels use; yet if I lack charity, I am no better than echoing bronze, or the clash of cymbals. I may have powers of prophecy, no secret hidden from me, no knowledge too deep for me; I may have utter faith, so that I can move mountains; yet if I lack charity, I count for nothing. I may give away all that I have, to feed the poor; I may give myself up to be burnt at the stake; if I lack charity, it goes for nothing (1 Cor. 13:1-2).

Charity means love: first of all, love for God above all things, and as a consequence love of our neighbour for God's sake. *Thou shalt love the Lord thy God with thy whole heart and thy whole soul and thy whole mind. This is the greatest of the commandments, and the first. And the second, its like, is this, Thou shalt love thy neighbour as thyself. On those two commandments, all the Law and the prophets depend* (Matt. 22:37-40).

But love is not only a question of sweet words and emotions. *My little children, let us show our love by the true test of action, not by taking phrases on our lips* (1 John 3:18). Love involves sacrifice, mortification. If we are not ready to deprive ourselves of something for the sake of God or the sake of others, our love is weak. *God has proved his love to us by laying down his life for our sakes; we too must be ready to lay down our lives for the sake of our brethren* (1 John 3:16). Love also implies obedience. St. John had deeply engraved in his soul the words of Jesus: *This is the greatest love a man can show: that he should lay down his life for his friends; and you, if you do all that I command you, are my friends* (John 15:13-14).

Unfortunately, many people choose to remember some of the things Jesus said and to forget others. The general commands of praying, of loving one another, of being sorry for one's sins, are accepted by all. The more specific precepts as to the way of fulfilling those commands are made the object of controversies. Yet to reject the Tradition of the Church, to refuse obedience to Peter's successors, to neglect the rites established by the Lord for the sanctification of the members of His Church, all this implies disobedience to Jesus. The Lord warned His disciples during the Last Supper: *If a man has any love for me, he will be true to my word; and then he will win my Father's love, and we will both come to him, and make our continual abode with him; whereas the man who has no love for me, lets my sayings pass him by* (John 14:23-24).

We let Jesus' sayings pass us by when we accept

some, but not all, of His teachings as they have been transmitted to us by the Apostles and their successors throughout the centuries.

St. Paul writes a beautiful hymn on the virtue of charity. *Charity is patient, is kind; charity feels no envy; charity is never perverse or proud; never insolent; does not claim its rights, cannot be provoked, does not brood over an injury; takes no pleasure in wrong-doing, but rejoices at the victory of truth; sustains, believes, hopes, endures to the last. The time will come when we shall outgrow prophecy, when speaking with tongues will come to an end, when knowledge will be swept away; we shall never have finished with charity* (1 Cor. 13:4-8).

This gift of love is accessible to all who seek it where it is to be found. *The love of God has been poured out in our hearts by the Holy Spirit, whom we have received* (Rom. 5:5).

Celibacy for the sake of the kingdom of God

> *At this his disciples said to him, If the case stands so between man and wife, it is better not to marry at all. That conclusion, he said, cannot be taken in by everybody, but only by those who have the gift. There are some eunuchs, who were so born from their mother's womb, some were made so by men, and some have made themselves so for love of the kingdom of heaven; take this in, you whose hearts are large enough for it* (Matt. 19:10-12).

The gift of celibacy for the sake of the Kingdom of Heaven is easily forgotten, perhaps because it is much more demanding and less *glorious* than other external gifts such as the gifts of tongues and of miracles. Yet it is truly a gift of God that cannot be lacking in His Church.

When the Lord spoke about the fundamental equality of women and men, the unity and indissolubility of marriage, the disciples protested: *If the case stands so between man and wife, it is better not to marry at all* (Matt. 19:10). Jesus did not correct such a statement, but rather confirmed it: yes, it is better not to marry, celibacy is a holier state of life, so much so that it cannot be achieved without a special gift from God: *That conclusion, he said, cannot be taken in by everybody, but only by those who have the gift* (Matt. 19:11).

Of course, celibacy involves total abstinence from sexual intercourse. There is no place in the kingdom of heaven for fornicators, adulterers and sinners against nature (cf. 1 Cor. 6:9-10). This is why the Lord illustrates his statement by talking about those who made themselves eunuchs for love of the kingdom of heaven. The fact that celibacy for God's sake is a gift of love is emphasised by the concluding remark of Christ: *take this in, you whose hearts are large enough for it* (Matt. 19:10-12).

When God told Adam and Eve: *Increase and multiply and fill the earth* (Gen. 1:28), He was giving a command to the human race in general, not to every human being that was to come into the world. He was not imposing on every man and woman a moral obligation to beget children, for earlier on He had said the same to the fish of the sea: *Increase and multiply, and fill the waters of the sea* (Gen. 1:22); the sea beasts were certainly not capable of assuming moral obligations. God's words were expressing His intention of making Man participate in His power of creation and were a formula of blessing upon all future generations.

The teaching of St. Paul leaves no room for doubt. *A man does well to abstain from all commerce with women* (1 Cor. 7:1). Marriage is good and is to be recommended in the majority of cases. *But, to avoid the danger of fornication, let every man keep his own wife, and every woman her own husband. Let every man give his wife what is her due, and every woman do the same by her husband; he, not she, claims the right over her body, as she, not he, claims the right over his. Do not starve one another, unless perhaps you do so for a time, by mutual consent, to have more freedom for prayer; come together again, or Satan will tempt you, weak as you are. I say this by way of concession; I am not imposing a rule on you* (1 Cor. 7:2-6).

Whether it is better for a particular person to marry or not to marry depends on the gift granted by God, although the gift of celibacy is to be held by all in high esteem. *I wish you were all in the same state as myself; but each of us has his own endowment from God, one to live in this way, another in that. To the unmarried, and to the widows, I would say that they will do well to remain in the same state as myself, but if they have not the gift of continence, let them marry; better to marry than to feel the heat of passion* (1 Cor. 7:7-10). It all depends on God's call, on the vocation He gives. *Everyone has his own vocation, in which he has been called; let him keep to it* (1 Cor. 7:20).

Marriage is holy, but celibacy for God's sake is holier still. Those whom God calls to marriage are called to be saints through their conjugal love. Those whom He calls to celibacy are called to be saints by a very special gift of love, and God claims from them all the love of their undivided hearts. *He who is unmarried is concerned with God's claim, asking how he is to please God; whereas the married man is concerned with the world's claim, asking how he is to please his wife; and thus he is at issue with himself. So a woman who is free of wedlock, or a virgin, is concerned with the Lord's claim, intent on holiness, bodily and spiritual; whereas the married woman is concerned with the world's claim, asking how she is to please her husband* (1 Cor. 7:32-34).

One sign of the active presence of the Holy Spirit in the Church is the abundance of this special gift of love, which was granted to Christians from the very beginning and without interruption up to the present day. St. Paul and St. John remained celibate, to be more free to preach the Good News. St. Agnes, St. Cecilia, St. Agatha, to mention just a few, preferred martyrdom rather than losing the glory of their virginity. Even in the darkest periods of the history of the Church, in the 9th and 10th centuries, the gift of celibacy was granted by God and joyfully taken up by generous souls such as St. Ansgar, who evangelised the Danes, Norwegians and Swedes, St. Cyril and St. Methodius, apostles of the Slavs, St. Adalbert of Magdeburg and St. Adalbert of Prague together with their monks, who converted whole nations in Central Europe. Later, the Cluny movement brought about a new blossoming of the life of full dedication to God. Nowadays too, great numbers of men and women respond to the Lord's call and give themselves entirely to Him as priests, religious, or ordinary lay people who renounce marriage in order to be more free to dedicate themselves to apostolic tasks. The gift of celibacy continues being found abundantly among the faithful followers of Christ who trust in His promise that *everyone who has forsaken home, or parents, or brethren, or wife, or children for the sake of the kingdom of God will receive, in this present world, many times their worth, and in the world to come, everlasting life* (Luke 18:29-30).

5

The Sanctifying Action of the Holy Spirit: III – Priests of Jesus Christ

So much I owe to the grace which God has given me, in making me a priest of Jesus Christ for the Gentiles, with God's gospel for my priestly charge, to make the Gentiles an offering worthy of acceptance, consecrated by the Holy Spirit (Rom 15:16).

The Apostles' ministry

When a man becomes a new creature in Christ, his old life has disappeared, everything has become new about him. This, as always, is God's doing; it is he who, through Christ, has reconciled us to himself, and allowed us to minister this reconciliation of his to others (2 Cor. 5:17-18).

In his Second Letter to the Corinthians, St. Paul speaks at length about his ministry. He addresses his readers, not as any Christian could address his fellow disciples, but as an Apostle who speaks in Christ's name and has been invested with His authority. By dying on the Cross, says Paul, Christ reconciled the world to Himself, but this reconciliation between God and each individual man is actually made effective through the ministry of the Apostles. God, *through Christ, has reconciled us to himself, and allowed us to minister this reconciliation of his to others* (2 Cor. 5:18). St. Paul insists on the dignity of the Apostles as representatives of Christ: *We are Christ's ambassadors, then, and God appeals to you through us; we entreat you in Christ's name, make your peace with God* (2 Cor. 5:20).

In this same letter, St. Paul describes the demands such a ministry imposes upon those who have received it: *We are careful not to give offence to anybody, lest we should bring discredit on our ministry; as God's ministers, we must do everything to make ourselves acceptable. We have to show great patience, in times of affliction, of need, of difficulty; under the lash, in prison, in the midst of tumult; when we are tired out, sleepless and fasting. We have to be pure-minded, enlightened, forgiving and gracious to others; we have to rely on the Holy Spirit, on unaffected love, on the truth of our message, on the power of God* (2 Cor. 6:3-7).

In Chapter Two we have already seen how Jesus Christ, while remaining the Supreme Shepherd, Judge, Teacher and King of God's People, entrusted His own authority to Peter and the other Apostles, and to their successors till the end of time, so that they should govern the Church in His name and lead all men to the knowledge of the Truth. The Apostles and their successors are empowered to act in the name of Christ, to represent Christ.

But Christ is not only Good Shepherd, Supreme Judge, Teacher and King. He is also Priest.

Jesus Christ, Eternal High Priest

> *Brethren and saints, you share a heavenly calling. Think, now, of Jesus as the apostle and the high priest of the faith which we profess* (Heb. 3:1).

When making His Covenant with Moses, God established the sons of Israel as His Chosen People. He also conferred the priesthood upon Aaron and his sons. *And now, that I may have priests to serve me among the Sons of Israel, summon thy brother Aaron, with his sons, Nadab, Asiu, Eleazar and Ithamar, to thy presence* (Ex. 28:1).

A priest is an intermediary between God and men, called by God through a special vocation. *The purpose for which any high priest is chosen from among his fellow men and made a representative of men in their dealings with God, is to offer gifts and sacrifices in expiation of their sins. He is qualified for this by being able to feel for them when they are ignorant and make mistakes, since he, too, is all beset with humiliations, and, for that reason, must needs present sin-offerings for himself, just as he does for the people. His vocation comes from God, as Aaron's did; nobody can take on himself such a privilege as this* (Heb. 5:1-4).

Christ possesses this priestly dignity in its fullness. *So it is with Christ. He did not raise himself to the dignity of the high priesthood; it was God that raised him to it, when he said, Thou art my Son, I have begotten thee this day, and so, elsewhere, Thou art a priest for ever, in the line of Melchisedech. Christ, during his earthly life, offered prayer and entreaty to the God who could save him from death, not without a piercing cry, not without tears; yet with such piety as won him a hearing. Son of God though he was, he learned obedience in the school of suffering, and now, his full achievement reached, he wins eternal salvation for all those who render obedience to him. A high priest in the line of Melchisedech, so God has called him* (Heb. 5:5-10).

The blood shed by Christ on the Cross was to seal a new covenant between God and men. This Jesus declared in the Last Supper: *This cup, he said, is the new testament, in my blood which is to be shed for you* (Luke 22:20). A new testament, or covenant, implied the formation of a new People and required a new priesthood and a new worship. *Now there could be no need for a fresh priest to arise, accredited with Melchisedech's priesthood, not with Aaron's, if the Levitical priesthood had brought fulfilment. And it is on the Levitical priesthood that the law given to God's people is founded. When the priesthood is altered, the law, necessarily, is altered with it. After all, he to whom the prophecy related belonged to a different tribe, which never produced a man to stand at the altar; our Lord took his origin from Juda, that is certain, and Moses in speaking of this tribe, said nothing about priests. And something further becomes evident, when a fresh priest arises to fulfil the type of Melchisedech, appointed, not to obey the law, with its outward observances, but in the power of an unending life. (Thou art a priest in the line of Melchisedech, God says of him, for ever.) The old observance is abrogated now, powerless as it was to help us; the law had nothing in it of final achievement. Instead, a fuller hope has been brought into our lives, enabling us to come close to God. And this time there is a ratification by oath; none was taken when those other priests were appointed, but the new priest is appointed with an oath, when God says to him, The Lord has sworn an irrevocable oath, Thou art a priest for ever; all the more solemn, then, is that covenant for which Jesus has been given us as our surety* (Heb. 7:11-22).

The new People of God embraces all men. The new Sacrifice is that of Jesus Christ on the Cross. The new Priest is Jesus Himself. Jesus is God, who acts both as Priest and Victim. Therefore the Victim is perfect, the Priest is sinless. A perfect Sacrifice has been offered, so fully acceptable and pleasing to God that it does not have to be repeated. There is only One Priest and One Sacrifice. *Of those other priests there was a succession, since death denied them permanence; whereas Jesus continues for ever, and his priestly office is unchanging; that is why he can give eternal salvation to those who through him make their way to God; he lives on still to make intercession on our behalf. Such was the high priest that suited our need, holy and guiltless and undefiled, not reckoned among us sinners, lifted high above all the heavens; one who has no need to do as those other priests did, offering a twofold sacrifice day by day, first for his own sins, then for those of the people. What he has done he has done once for all; and the offering was himself. The law makes high priests of men, and men are frail; promise and oath, now, have superseded the law; our high priest, now, is that Son who has reached his full achievement for all eternity* (Heb. 7:23-28).

The Sacrifice of the Cross

> *As Christ comes into the world, he says, No sacrifice, no offering was thy demand; thou hast endowed me, instead, with a body. Thou has not found any pleasure in burnt-sacrifices, in sacrifices for sin. See then, I said, I am coming to fulfil what is written of me, where the book lies unrolled; to do thy will, O my God* (Heb. 10:5-7).

The sacrifices of bulls and goats were unable to purify men from their sins. *No, what these offerings bring with them, year by year, is only the remembrance of sins; that sins should be taken away by the blood of bulls and goats is impossible* (Heb. 10:3-4). Only a perfect sacrifice could effect the reconciliation of men with God, and this is what Jesus Christ achieved. *In accordance with this divine will we have been sanctified by an offering made once for all, the body of Jesus Christ. One high priest after another must stand there, day after day, offering again and again the same sacrifices, which can never take away our sins; whereas he sits for ever at the right hand of God, offering for our sins a sacrifice that is never repeated. He only waits, until all his enemies are made a footstool under his feet; by a single offering he has completed his work, for all time, in those whom he sanctifies* (Heb. 10:10-14).

It is worth reading attentively the chapters 5 to 10 of the Letter to the Hebrews. The inspired writer insists on the unique, unrepeatable Sacrifice of Christ and His unending, permanent and exclusive Priesthood.

On the one hand, the sacred texts tell us: *nor does he make a repeated offering of himself, as the high priest, when he enters the sanctuary, makes a yearly offering of the blood that is not his own. If that were so, he must have suffered again and again, ever since the world was created; as it is, he has been revealed once for all, at the moment when history reached its fulfilment, annulling our sin by his sacrifice. Man's destiny is to die once for all; nothing remains after that but judgement; and Christ was offered once for all, to drain the cup of a world's sins* (Heb. 9:25-28).

On the other hand, the prophet Malachias announced a perfect sacrifice that would be offered to God constantly and everywhere. *No corner of the world, from sun's rise to sun's setting, where the renown of me is not heard among the Gentiles, where sacrifice is not done, and pure offering made in my honour; so revered is my name, says the Lord of hosts, there among the Gentiles* (Mal. 1:11). Here the Holy Spirit, speaking through the prophet, is evidently not referring to a Jewish sacrifice, for the whole prophecy of Malachias is a strong rebuke to the Levites and their offerings.

What is this perpetual and perfect sacrifice announced by the Prophet? How is it compatible with the One Sacrifice offered once for all by Jesus Christ on the Altar of the Cross?

The Sacrifice of the Altar

> *The Tradition which I received from the Lord, and handed on to you, is that the Lord Jesus, on the night when he was betrayed, took bread, and gave thanks, and broke it, and said, Take, eat; this is my body, given up for you. Do this for a commemoration of me. And so with the cup, when supper was ended, This cup, he said, is the new testament, in my blood. Do this, whenever you drink it, for a commemoration of me. So it is the Lord's death that you are heralding, whenever you eat this bread and drink this cup, until he comes* (1 Cor. 11:23-26).

In Capharnaum, Jesus spoke about the bread of life He would give to the world. That bread was Himself. *It is I who am the bread of life* (John 6:35). The Jews were shocked by such a statement coming from a village carpenter. Jesus insisted on His teaching. *I myself am the living bread that has come down from heaven. If anyone eats of this bread, he shall live for ever. And now, what is this bread which I am to give? It is my flesh, given for the life of the world* (John 6:51-52).

It is easy to imagine the surprise and even the feeling of repulsion many of His hearers experienced, imagining that Jesus was suggesting some sort of human sacrifice followed by acts of cannibalism. But the Lord did not modify His teaching. *Believe me when I tell you this; you can have no life in yourselves, unless*

*you eat the flesh of the Son of Man, and drink his blood.
The man who eats my flesh and drinks my blood enjoys
eternal life, and I will raise him up at the last day. My
flesh is real food, my blood is real drink. He who eats my
flesh and drinks my blood, lives continually in me, and I
in him. As I live because of the Father, the living Father
who has sent me, so he who eats me will live, in his turn,
because of me* (John 6:54-58).

Jesus was not speaking only in parables, in à
figurative sense. We see in other passages of the Bible
what happened when He spoke to the crowds in
parables: to the people *he spoke only in parables, and
made all plain to his disciples when they were alone*
(Mark 4:34). The Apostles would not have deceived
themselves for long. It is interesting to compare the
attitude of Jesus in Capharnaum with his attitude on
other occasions when He had been using figurative
language.

One day Jesus exclaimed in the presence of the
multitude: *Listen to this and grasp what it means. It is
not what goes into a man's mouth that makes him
unclean; what makes a man unclean is what comes out
of his mouth* (Matt. 15:10-11). If we take these words
literally, they are indeed shocking. It is not surprising
that the disciples should tell the Lord: *Dost thou know
that the Pharisees, when they heard thy saying, took it
amiss?* (Matt. 15:12). At the request of Peter, Jesus
explained what He had meant: *What, he said, are you
still without wits? Do you not observe that any
uncleanness which finds its way into a man's mouth
travels down into his belly, and so is cast into the sewer;
whereas all that comes out of his mouth comes from the
heart, and it is that which makes a man unclean? It is*

from the heart that his wicked designs come, his sins of murder, adultery, fornication, theft, perjury and blasphemy. It is these make a man unclean; he is not made unclean by eating without washing his hands (Matt. 15:16-20).

In other words, Jesus explained to his disciples: do not take my words literally, but see the spiritual meaning behind the allegory.

On another occasion, *they crossed the sea, and his disciples found that they had forgotten to take bread with them. So when Jesus said to them, See that you have nothing to do with the leaven of the Pharisees and Sadducees, they were anxious in their minds; We have brought no bread, they said. Jesus knew it, and said to them, Men of little faith, what is this anxiety in your minds, that you have brought no bread with you? Have you no wits even now, or have you forgotten the five thousand and their five loaves, and the number of baskets you filled? Or the four thousand and their seven loaves, and the number of hampers you filled then? How could you suppose that I was thinking of bread, when I said, Have nothing to do with the leaven of the Pharisees and Sadducees? Then they understood that his warning was against the doctrine of the Pharisees and Sadducees, not against leavened bread* (Matt. 16:5-12). So Jesus always helped His disciples to understand the true meaning of His words.

In Capharnaum, in His discourse on the Bread of Life, Jesus reacted in a different way. He had spoken very hard words: *You can have no life in yourselves, unless you eat the flesh of the Son of Man, and drink his blood* (John 6:54). When His hearers protested, saying *this is strange talk, who can be expected to listen to it?*

(John 6:61), Jesus did not try to explain the true meaning of His words, for He had said the plain truth. He only affirmed the necessity to receive His teaching with faith, trusting in divine revelation (the spirit) rather than in human wisdom (the flesh). *Does this try your faith? What will you make of it, if you see the Son of Man ascending to the place where he was before? Only the spirit gives life; the flesh is of no avail; and the words I have been speaking to you are spirit, and life. But there are some, even among you, who do not believe* (John 6:63-65). Many disciples left Him then. When Jesus addressed the Twelve, it was not to explain the parable for there was none. *Whereupon Jesus said to the twelve, Would you too, go away?* (John 6:68) It was a way of telling them: I meant exactly what I said, and there are only two alternatives: to accept my words, or to abandon me.

During the Last Supper, when *Jesus took bread, and blessed, and broke it, and gave it to his disciples, saying, Take, eat, this is my body* (Matt. 26:26), and then *took a cup, and offered thanks, and gave it to them, saying, Drink, all of you, of this; for this is my blood, of the new testament, shed for many, to the remission of sins* (Matt. 26:27-28), the Apostles must have remembered that day in Capharnaum, and seen in what a wonderful and simple way the Lord's announcement was being fulfilled: *My flesh is real food, my blood is real drink* (John 6:56).

Not only did Jesus give His Apostles His body to eat and His blood to drink on this particular occasion. He also gave them power to do the same thing for the benefit of all Christians: *Do this for a commemoration of me* (Luke 22:19). The Apostles were to lend their hands and voice to Christ until the end of time, saying in His name: *This is my body; this is my blood*, and thereby transforming bread and wine into the true substance of the body and blood of the Lord.

Christians understood very well this command of Jesus to perpetuate His one and only Sacrifice. From the very beginning, *they occupied themselves continually with the apostles' teaching, their fellowship in the breaking of bread, and the fixed times of prayer* (Acts 2:42). Many years later, St. Paul wrote to the Corinthians about the celebration of the Mass: *The tradition which I received from the Lord, and handed on to you, is that the Lord Jesus, on the night when he was being betrayed, took bread, and gave thanks, and broke it, and said, Take, eat; this is my body, given up for you. Do this for a commemoration of me. So it is the Lord's death that you are heralding, whenever you eat this bread and drink this cup, until he comes* (1 Cor. 11:23-26). St. Paul makes it clear that there is no new sacrifice; instead the one Sacrifice of the Cross, in which Jesus died for us, is made present on the altar. It is not a representation (which means a simple symbol) but a re-presentation of the saving death of Jesus Christ as the true body and blood of the Lord are made present and are offered in the Mass. *And therefore, if anyone eats this bread or drinks this cup of the Lord unworthily, he will be held to account for the Lord's body and blood. A man must examine himself first, and then eat of that bread and drink of that cup; he is eating and drinking damnation to himself if he eats and drinks unworthily, not recognising the Lord's body for what it is* (1 Cor. 11:27-29).

Those words of St. Paul are very strong. A man

who participates in a simple commemorative celebration without the right dispositions of heart can be accused of hypocrisy, but not of murder, while St. Paul's words imply a very direct attack upon the Lord's body, with the shedding of His blood. The Apostle's teaching is clear: we must recognise the consecrated bread for what it is: the body of the Lord.

It is interesting to note that St. Paul states the supernatural origin of Christian Tradition: it is not a simple transmission of beliefs from generation to generation, but first of all a teaching received from Christ Himself, which is then preserved and transmitted in all its integrity through the teaching of the Church. *The tradition which I received from the Lord, and handed on to you, is ...* No man, therefore, has the authority to modify it.

Thou art a priest for ever, in the line of Melchisedech (Heb. 5:6), Sacred Scripture says of Christ who is *a high priest, now, eternally with the priesthood of Melchisedech* (Heb. 6:20). Melchisedech was a figure of Jesus Christ, because he was a priest without human origin (the Book of Genesis mentions no genealogy, gives no explanation about Melchisedech, king of Salem). *That is all; no name of father or mother, no pedigree, no date of birth or of death; there he stands, eternally, a priest, the true figure of the Son of God* (Heb. 7:3). What kind of sacrifice did Melchisedech offer? *He, priest as he was of the most high God, brought out bread and wine with him, and gave him this benediction, On Abram be the blessing of the most high God, maker of heaven and earth* (Gen. 14:18-19).

So Melchisedech offered a sacrifice of bread and

wine. Christ is a priest in the line of Melchisedech. We know that He offered His own body as a sacrifice for the remission of sin. What is the connection between the sacrifice of Christ and the sacrifice of Melchisedech? The Gospels give us the answer: *and while they were still at table, Jesus took bread, and blessed, and broke it, and gave it to his disciples, saying, Take, eat, this is my body. Then he took a cup, and offered thanks, and gave it to them, saying, Drink, all of you, of this; for this is my blood, of the new testament, shed for many, to the remission of sins. And I tell you this, I shall not drink of this fruit of the vine again, until I drink it with you, new wine, in the kingdom of my Father* (Matt. 26:26-29). The Sacrifice of the Cross is re-presented to us in the offering of bread and wine that are transformed, through Christ's power, into the Lord's own body and blood.

And so the prophecy of Malachias continues being fulfilled after nearly 2000 years of the Christian era: a pure sacrifice, a perfect offering is made in all corners of the world, from sunrise to sunset. As the sun is constantly rising or setting somewhere in the world, there is no moment when a Mass is not being celebrated in some corner of the earth. Yet there is only one Sacrifice, that of the Cross; one Victim, Jesus Christ; one Priest, the Saviour, who lets His voice be heard among men through the ministry of His representatives, sharers in his own Priesthood.

The priestly ministry

> *Fix thy mind on Jesus Christ, sprung from the race of David, who has risen from the dead; that is the gospel I preach, and in its service I suffer hardship like a criminal, yes, even imprisonment; but there is no imprisoning the word of God. For its sake I am ready to undergo anything; for love of the elect, that they, like us, may win salvation in Christ Jesus, and eternal glory with it* (2 Tim. 2:8-10).

A priest acts in the name and the person of Christ and must truly represent Christ among men. The principal activities of Jesus in His Public Life were preaching, proving the truth of His teachings through the miracles He performed; forgiving sins, bringing men to repentance and to friendship with God; and offering His Supreme Sacrifice, followed by His glorious Resurrection and Ascension into heaven, entrusting to His Church the evangelisation of the world.

And so the priests who share in the Priesthood of Christ must preach: *And he said to them, Go out all over the world and preach the gospel to the whole of creation* (Mark 16:15). Even corporal works of mercy are to be placed in second position: *It is too much that we should have to forgo preaching God's word, and bestow our care upon tables* (Acts 6:2), the Apostles exclaimed when they saw the need for a better organisation of charitable works. St. Paul expresses very clearly the grave duty imposed by Christ upon His

Ministers: *When I preach the Gospel, I take no credit for that; I act under constraint; it would go hard with me indeed if I did not preach the gospel. I can claim a reward for what I do of my own choice; but when I act under constraint, I am only executing a commission* (1 Cor. 9:16-17).

Jesus had power to forgive sins. *And Jesus, seeing their faith, said to the palsied man, Son, thy sins are forgiven. But there were some of the scribes sitting there, who reasoned in their mind, Why does he speak so? He is talking blasphemously. Who can forgive sins but God, and God only? Jesus knew at once, in his spirit, of these secret thoughts of theirs, and said to them, Why do you reason thus in your minds? Which command is more lightly given, to say to the palsied man, Thy sins are forgiven, or to say, Rise up, take thy bed with thee, and walk? And now, to convince you that the Son of Man has authority to forgive sins while he is on earth (here he spoke to the palsied man): I tell thee, rise up, take thy bed with thee, and go home* (Mark 2:5-11). After His Resurrection, Jesus entrusted to His Apostles His own authority to continue His Mission. *Once more Jesus said to them, Peace be upon you; I came upon an errand from my Father, and now I am sending you out in my turn. With that he breathed on them, and said to them, Receive the Holy Spirit; when you forgive men's sins, they are forgiven, when you hold them bound, they are held bound* (John 20:21-23). God's priests therefore have authority to forgive sins in the name of Christ.

Jesus commanded His Apostles to renew in a mysterious, sacramental way, the Sacrifice of His own Body and Blood, when He told them: *Do this for a commemoration of me*. He sent them to baptise with water and the Holy Spirit. He established an Anointing to give both spiritual and bodily strength to the sick. Already, when the Apostles were sent to preach, two by two, in the villages, *they cast out many devils, and many who were sick they anointed with oil, and healed them* (Mark 6:13). Years later, St. James bore witness of the existence of a rite performed by the priests for the benefit of the sick: *Is one of you sick? Let him send for the presbyters of the church, and let them pray over him, anointing him with oil in the Lord's name. Prayer offered in faith will restore the sick man, and the Lord will give him relief; if he is guilty of sins, they will be pardoned* (James 5:14-15).

And St. Paul could truly say that it is God *who through Christ, has reconciled us to himself, and allowed us to minister this reconciliation of his to others* (2 Cor. 5:18).

Ministerial priesthood and common priesthood of the faithful

> *He has proved his love for us, by washing us clean from our sins in his own blood, and made us a royal race of priests, to serve God his Father* (Apoc. 1:5-6).

There is no contradiction between the fact that God calls certain persons to share in His Priesthood, and the fact that the Christian people forms a royal priesthood. Indeed, the term *priesthood* can be taken in two different meanings. The Old Testament provides a key to the distinction between both concepts.

In the first chapters of the Book of Leviticus, we read the regulations laid down by God for the offering of sacrifices. Only in the case of a peace-offering may the giver of the victim partake in the sacrificial meal (cf. Lev. 7:11-21). Normally, only members of the priestly family may eat of the sacred offerings. *No-one that is not of their family may share the holy food, no guest the priest entertains, no hired servant of his; only a slave bought with his money or born in his house has the privilege. If a priest's daughter marries out of her clan, she loses her right to these hallowed offerings; but if she becomes a widow, or is rejected by her husband and comes home childless, she may eat with her family as when she was still a maid. It is only those who belong to another clan that may not share it* (Lev. 22:10-13). Even when a man of the priestly clan was disqualified from the exercise of the priesthood (the offering of sacrifices), he could still partake of sacred offerings: *No-one of the priestly line of Aaron who has such a blemish must come forward to sacrifice to the Lord, or offer his God the consecrated loaves. He is allowed to eat the bread which is offered in the sanctuary, but he must have no access to the veil, must not go near the altar; my sanctuary must not be profaned by any blemish. I, the Lord, have set priests apart for myself* (Lev. 21:21-23). The distinction is made between the priestly ministry and the dignity of member of the priestly clan.

In the Church established by Jesus Christ, priests are set aside to carry out sacred functions, especially that of offering the Holy Sacrifice of the Mass, which is nothing else but the Sacrifice of the Cross made present to men throughout the centuries. They are also the official preachers of the Church. All other members of the Church form a priestly people because they are called to unite themselves to the Sacrifice of Christ, to share in it by partaking of the Body of the Lord, and to make Christ known to others. *You are a chosen race, a royal priesthood, a consecrated nation, a people God means to have for himself; it is yours to proclaim the exploits of the God who has called you out of darkness into his marvellous light* (1 Peter 2:9). *So it is the Lord's death that you are heralding, whenever you eat this bread and drink this cup, until he comes* (1 Cor. 11:26).

Old Testament priests were chosen from among Aaron's descendants, who formed a priestly clan within God's People. New Testament priests are chosen from among the baptised people, who have become children of God, brothers of Jesus Christ, members of God's family. Therefore the members of the Church form a race of priests (cf. Apoc. 1:6), but only through a special calling does a man receive the ministerial priesthood.

The Christian people exercise their common priesthood by participating in the Sacrifice of the Mass, praying for others and doing apostolate. *Stand fast, your loins girt with truth, the breastplate of justice fitted on, and your feet shod in readiness to publish the gospel of peace. With all this, take up the shield of faith, with which you will be able to quench all the fire-tipped arrows of your wicked enemy; make the helmet of salvation your own, and the sword of the spirit, God's word. Use every kind of prayer and supplication; pray at all times in the spirit; keep awake to that end with all perseverance; offer your supplication for all the saints. Pray for me, too, that I may be given words to speak my mind boldly, in making known the gospel revelation, for which I am an ambassador in chains; that I may have boldness to speak as I ought* (Eph. 6:14-20).

St. John tells us: *The Holy One has anointed you, and now nothing is hidden from you* (1 John 2:20). In Old Testament times, priests and kings used to be anointed as a sign of a special choice from God and of a *setting apart* of a man for a sacred function. The Book of Leviticus tells us how not only priests, but also all objects dedicated to the worship of God were anointed: *Then he took the oil used for anointing, and with it he anointed the tabernacle and all its furniture; anointed the altar, too, after consecrating it seven times by sprinkling, with all its appurtenances, and consecrated the basin and its stand with oil. Then, pouring oil over Aaron's head, he anointed and hallowed him* (Lev. 8:10-12). Samuel anointed Saul to make him king over God's people: *And now Samuel took out his phial of oil, and poured it out over Saul's head; then he kissed him, and said, Hereby the Lord anoints thee to be the leader of his chosen people* (1 Kings 10:1).

This explains why Jesus was also called Christ (which means *Anointed* – as does the title *Messiah*) for He was to be Eternal Priest (cf. Heb. 7:24) and King of a Kingdom that would have no end (cf. Luke 1:33). It also sheds light on the royal priesthood common to the Christian people. The ceremonies of Baptism include an anointing with oil; in Confirmation the Bishop lays his hand on the head of a Christian while anointing him with chrism; when a man is ordained priest, the Bishop anoints his hands that will be *lent* to Christ to hold the Body of the Lord and distribute God's blessings; finally, when the moment approaches to appear before

God's Tribunal, the Christian is made ready for Heaven through a last anointing, the Anointing of the Sick. Truly could St. Paul say: *It is God who gives both us and you our certainty in Christ; it is he who has anointed us, just as it is he who has put his seal on us, and given us the foretaste of his Spirit in our hearts* (2 Cor. 1:21-22).

Women and priesthood

> *And women are to be silent in the churches; utterance is not permitted to them; let them keep their rank, as the law tells them: if they have any question to raise, let them ask their husbands at home. That a woman should make her voice heard in the church is not seemly* (1 Cor. 14:34-35).

It is interesting to note that the Holy Spirit, speaking through St. Paul, commands women to be silent in the churches. Yet Christianity is not a religion that places the woman in a position of inferiority. Jesus granted Jewish women the title of *daughters of Abraham* (cf. Luke 13:16), unlike the Jews who only acknowledged men as sons of Abraham. He performed miracles for many women; He taught them about the kingdom of God. He chose women as the first messengers of His Resurrection. He closely associated His Mother to His work of Redemption.

St. Paul did not forbid women to exercise such

gifts as prophecy: *A woman brings shame upon her head if she uncovers it to pray or prophesy* (1 Cor. 11:5). So a woman may prophesy with her head covered; but she is not to do so in the churches in an official capacity. She cannot, therefore, act as an official representative of Christ, i.e. be called to the priesthood.

Jesus manifested His intention to call only men to the priesthood by choosing twelve men as His Apostles and sending them to preach, to baptise, to forgive sins, to transform bread and wine into His own Body and Blood. He so acted, not because of the prejudices prevailing in His times, but because He chose to. The concept of women as religious leaders was not unknown to the people of Christ's lifetime: many pagan religions had women as priestesses, and the people of Israel would not have forgotten that they had, in the times of Judges, been ruled by a woman: *At this time Israel was ruled by a prophetess called Debora, the wife of Lapidoth, that dwelt in the hill-country of Ephraim, between Rama and Bethel, by that palm-tree which long bore her name; here the people of Israel had recourse to her for the settlement of all their disputes* (Judges 4:4-5). Under Debora's leadership the enemy of Israel, Sisara, was killed by a woman, Jahel, who received the praise of her people: *Here were men that would not rally in the Lord's cause, would not come to aid his champions in their peril. But Jahel, wife of Haber the Cinite, blessed may she be above all women; a blessing on the tent she dwells in!* (Judges 5:23-24).

Jesus welcomed the assistance of women in His public Ministry. *With him were the twelve apostles, and certain women, whom he had freed from evil spirits and from sicknesses, Mary who is called Magdalen, who had*

had seven devils cast out of her, and Joanna, the wife of Chusa, Herod's steward, and Susanna, and many others, who ministered to him with the means they had (Luke 8:2-3). Yet these were not called to the priesthood. He did not confer the priesthood even to His own Mother, the *blessed among women* (Luke 1:28), the one who had *found favour in the sight of God* (Luke 1:30), who was blessed for her believing (cf. Luke 1:45).

Women share in the common priesthood of the faithful. Only the ministerial priesthood is reserved for men, because priests, in the exercise of their ministry, act not in their own person but in the person of Christ. Since Christ is a man, not a woman, He is more perfectly represented by a man. This point can be argued. But one fact remains: no woman was admitted by Christ as an Apostle, the Apostles in their turn followed the example of their Master, and their successors felt the need of remaining faithful to this tradition received from Christ and from the first Christians. Not even a man can appoint himself as a priest; he has no *right* to the priesthood but must be called: *his vocation comes from God, as Aaron's did; nobody can take on himself such a privilege as this* (Heb. 5:4). As neither Christ nor the Apostles called women to the priesthood, women simply *cannot* be priests.

In case our pride makes it hard for us to accept this teaching as coming from God Himself, St. Paul affirms: *If anybody claims to be a prophet, or to have spiritual gifts, let him prove it by recognising that this message of mine is God's commandment. If he does not recognise it, he himself shall receive no recognition* (1 Cor. 14:37-38).

.

6

Liberation from Sin

In the Son of God, in his blood, we find the redemption that sets us free from our sins (Col. 1:14)

True purification from sins

It is a holy God who has called you, and you too must be holy in all the ordering of your lives; you must be holy, the scripture says, because I am holy (1 Peter 1:15-16).

An angel had announced to Joseph that the Child to be born of Mary would free us from sin: *and she will bear a son, whom thou shalt call Jesus, for he is to save his people from their sins* (Matt. 1:21). John the Baptist bore witness to the saving mission of Christ: *Look, this is he who takes away the sin of the world* (John 1:29). The Lord Himself promised true freedom, freedom from sin, to His disciples: *If you continue faithful to my word, you are my disciples in earnest, and the truth will set you free. They answered him, We are of Abraham's breed, nobody ever enslaved us yet; what dost thou mean by saying, You shall become free? And Jesus answered them, Believe me when I tell you this; everyone who acts sinfully is the slave of sin, and the slave cannot make his home in the house for ever. To make his home in the house for ever, is for the Son. Why then, if it is the Son who makes you free men, you will have freedom in earnest* (John 8:31-36). This implies a real liberation from the power of the devil and the slavery of sin.

The man who lives sinfully takes his character from the devil, St. John tells us (1 John 3:7). The Lord Himself had explained how sinful acts defile a man: *it is from the heart that his wicked designs come, his sins of murder, adultery, fornication, theft, perjury and blasphemy. It is these make a man unclean; he is not made unclean by eating without washing his hands* (Matt. 15:19-20). But what stains a pagan stains a Christian as well; what is sinful for a pagan is also sinful for a Christian, and so our salvation implies a healing of the wound produced by sin in our nature, and the capacity to avoid sin and to perform supernaturally good actions. *Yes, brethren, freedom claimed you when you were called. Only, do not let this freedom give a foothold to corrupt nature; you must be servants still, serving one another in a spirit of charity* (Gal. 5:13).

There is no foundation in the Bible for Luther's teaching on the total corruption of human nature and the impossibility of avoiding sinful acts. According to Luther, man's nature remains sinful but Christ's merits cover up and hide such sinfulness as by a cloak. Such a theory is not acceptable in the light of St. Paul's words:

Let me say this; learn to live and move in the spirit; then there is no danger of your giving way to the impulses of corrupt nature. The impulses of nature and the impulses of the spirit are at war with one another; either is clean contrary to the other, and that is why you cannot do all that your will approves. It is by letting the spirit lead you that you free yourselves from the yoke of the law. It is easy to see what effects proceed from corrupt nature; they are such things as adultery, impurity, incontinence, luxury, idolatry, witchcraft, feuds, quarrels, jealousies, outbursts of anger, rivalries, dissensions, factions, spite, murder, drunkenness, and debauchery. I warn you, as I have warned you before, that those who live in such a way will not inherit God's kingdom. Whereas the spirit yields a harvest of love, joy, peace, patience, kindness, generosity, forbearance, gentleness, faith, courtesy, temperateness, purity. No law can touch lives such as these; those who belong to Christ have crucified nature, with all its passions, all its impulses. Since we live by the spirit, let the spirit be our rule of life (Gal. 5:16-25).

When St. Peter says that *charity draws the veil over a multitude of sins*, he means that charity attracts God's forgiveness, causing a multitude of sins to be washed away; Jesus taught us this when he forgave the sinful woman in the house of Simon the Pharisee: *Dost thou see this woman? I came into thy house, and thou gavest me no water for my feet; she has washed my feet with her tears, and wiped them with her hair. Thou gavest me no kiss of greeting; she has never ceased to kiss my feet since I entered; thou didst not pour oil on my head; she has anointed my feet, and with ointment. And so, I tell thee, if great sins have been forgiven her, she has also greatly loved. He loves little, who has little forgiven him. Then he said to her, Thy sins are forgiven* (Luke 7:44-48).

To make it clear that Christ saved us not only from hell itself, but from the deeds deserving of hell, St. Paul warned us against false teachers in this respect: *This you must know well enough, that nobody can claim a share in Christ's kingdom, God's kingdom, if he is debauched, or impure, or has that love of money which makes man an idolater. Do not allow any man to cheat you with empty promises; these are the very things which bring down God's anger on the unbelievers; you do ill to throw in your lot with them* (Eph. 5:5-7).

First purification from sin: Baptism

> *We have died, once for all, to sin; can we breathe its air again? You know well enough that we who were taken up into Christ by baptism have been taken up, all of us, into his death. In our baptism we have been buried with him, died like him, that so, just as Christ was raised up by his Father's power from the dead, we too might live and move in a new kind of existence* (Rom. 6:2-4).

This liberation from sin, Jesus won it for us by His Passion and Death: *Enemies of God, we were reconciled to him through his Son's death; reconciled to him, we are surer than ever of finding salvation in his Son's life. And, what is more, we can boast of God's protection; always through our Lord Jesus Christ, since it is through him that we have attained our reconciliation* (Rom. 5:10-11).

For this reconciliation to be made effective, each individual person must unite himself to the death and resurrection of Christ, and this is done through Baptism. In the 6th chapter of his Letter to the Romans, St. Paul declares: *You know well enough that we who were taken up into Christ by baptism have been taken up, all of us, into his death* (Rom. 6:3). And he goes on explaining how the baptised Christian has died and risen with Christ, and lives a new life in the service of God, having rejected sin. *We have to be closely fitted into the pattern of his resurrection, as we have been into the pattern of his death; we have to be sure of this, that our former nature has been crucified with him, and the living power of our guilt annihilated, so that we are the slaves of guilt no longer. Guilt makes no more claim on a man who is dead. And if we have died with Christ, we have faith to believe that we shall share his life* (Rom. 6:5-8). The whole chapter deals with this death to sin, this liberation from sin, which is the result of our Baptism. St Paul knew well the need and the effects of baptism. He never forgot God's message to him through Ananias in Damascus: Rise up, and receive Baptism, washing away thy sins at the invocation of his name (Acts 22:16).

St. Peter also speaks of this liberation from sin through Baptism. *What was the ransom that freed you from the vain observances of ancestral tradition? You know well enough that it was not paid in earthly currency, silver or gold; it was paid in the precious blood of Christ; no lamb was ever so pure, so spotless a victim . . . ; through him you have learned to be faithful to God, who raised him up from the dead and endowed him with*

*glory; your faith and your hope are to be centred in God.
Purify your souls with the discipline of charity ... since
you have all been born anew with an immortal,
imperishable birth, through the words of God who lives
and abides for ever* (1 Peter 1:18-23). This immortal,
imperishable birth is none other than the new birth
from water and the Holy Spirit announced by Jesus to
Nicodemus.

Baptism washes away our sins by conferring us
sanctifying grace, i.e. a share in God's own life, so that
the Holy Spirit may dwell in our souls.

Christ died for all men, and therefore He won
salvation for all and His grace is made available to all.
*The grace of God, our Saviour, has dawned on all men
alike* (Titus 2:11). Yet, in order to be saved, a person
must find faith in Christ and unite himself to His Death
and Resurrection through Baptism. *In accordance to
his own merciful design he saved us, with the cleansing
power which gives us new birth, and restores our nature
through the Holy Spirit, shed on us in abundant measure
through our Saviour Jesus Christ. So, justified by his
grace, we were to become heirs, with the hope of eternal
life set before us* (Titus 3:5-7).

God's gift of grace

> *Our sins had made dead men of us, and
> he, in giving his life to Christ, gave life to
> us too; it is his grace that has saved you;
> raised us up too, enthroned us too above
> the heavens, in Christ Jesus. He would*

*have all future ages see, in that clemency
which he showed us in Christ Jesus, the
surpassing richness of his grace. Yes, it
was grace that saved you, with faith for its
instrument; it did not come from
yourselves, it was God's gift, not from any
action of yours, or there would be room
for pride. No, we are his design; God has
created us in Christ Jesus, pledged to such
good actions as he has prepared
beforehand, to be the employment of our
lives* (Eph. 2:5-10).

In the same way as the Acts of the Apostles have
sometimes been called *the Gospel of the Holy Spirit*
because of the abundant references made to the action
of the Holy Spirit in the life of the Church, the Epistles
of St. Paul could be grouped under the title "Gospel of
God's grace".

The word *grace* corresponds to the Greek word
Χαρις (charis) or Χαρισμα (charisma – special
grace). It means *favour*; but as the English word *grace*
also means *favour*, no-one should object to the
translation of Χαρις as grace. To look graciously upon
someone is to look favourably upon him. To grant a
grace is to grant a favour. An act of grace is a favour
granted freely, not as a right. To fall from grace is to
fall out of favour. Many more examples could be given.
These are enough to understand that the Christian
concept of grace means a free gift from God granted as
an undeserved favour, as expressed by St. Paul in the
above-quoted passage.

The greeting *The grace of our Lord Jesus Christ be*

with you (1 Cor. 16:24; 1 Thess. 5:28) used with slight variants by St. Paul, St. Peter and St. John could be translated as: *The favour of our Lord Jesus Christ be with you*, with the danger of understanding it as a general benevolent feeling of Christ towards His disciples. In other passages, however, it is clear that this *favour* is not simply a *favourable feeling* that dwells only in the person from whom it originates (in this case God), while being motivated by some attractive quality in the person who is the object of it. *The grace of the Lord came upon me in a full tide of faith and love, the love that is in Christ Jesus* (1 Tim. 1:14): this grace is a gift received by man, bringing with it the theological virtues of Faith, Hope and Charity that make it possible to know God as He truly is and love Him in a supernatural way. It is called *sanctifying grace*.

The Letter of St. Paul to the Romans can be described as a short treatise on the grace of God through which we are justified. First, St. Paul speaks about the way God carried out our justification, *God's way of justification through faith in Jesus Christ, meant for everybody and sent down upon everybody without distinction, if he has faith. All alike have sinned, all alike are unworthy of God's praise. And justification comes to us as a free gift from his grace, through our redemption in Christ Jesus* (Rom. 3:22-24). This justification consists in the gift of sanctifying grace, granted by God to erase the sin of Adam (original sin) with which all men are born: *Only, the grace which came to us was out of all proportion to the fault. If this one man's fault brought death on a whole multitude, all the more lavish was God's grace, shown to a whole multitude, that free gift he made us in the grace brought by one man, Jesus Christ.*

The extent of the gift is not as if it followed a single guilty act; the sentence which brought us condemnation arose out of one man's action, whereas the pardon that brings us acquittal arises out of a multitude of faults. And if death began its reign through one man, owing to one man's fault, more fruitful still is the grace, the gift of justification, which bids men enjoy a reign of life through one man, Jesus Christ (Rom. 5, 15-17). And the Apostle exclaims: *as our fault was amplified, grace has been more amply bestowed than ever; that so, where guilt held its reign of death, justifying grace should reign instead, to bring us eternal life through Jesus Christ our Lord* (Rom. 5:20-21).

Only God's grace can enable us to overcome the sinful tendencies of our nature wounded (but not totally corrupted) by sin. *Pitiable creature that I am, who is to set me free from a nature thus doomed to death? Nothing else than the grace of God, through Jesus Christ our Lord* (Rom. 7:24-25).

In the chapter 8 of the Letter to the Romans, St. Paul describes the effects of sanctifying grace. Though he does not pronounce the word *grace*, the comparison he makes between *life of nature* and *life of the spirit* must be understood in the context of the preceding chapters. Sanctifying grace is a supernatural gift that abides in our soul: *but you live the life of the spirit, not the life of nature; that is, if the Spirit of God dwells in you* (Rom. 8:9). It makes us holy, having justified us in God's sight: *He has signed the death-warrant of sin in our nature, so that we should be fully quit of the law's claim, we, who follow the way of the spirit, not the ways of flesh and blood* (Rom. 8:3-4). Grace makes us, not only friends of God, but God's own children, brothers of Jesus Christ and heirs of heaven: *Those who follow the leading of God's spirit are all God's sons; the spirit you have now received is not, as of old, a spirit of slavery, to govern you by fear; it is the spirit of adoption, which makes us cry out, Abba, Father. The Spirit himself thus assures our spirit, that we are children of God; and if we are his children, then we are his heirs too; heirs of God, sharing the inheritance of Christ; only we must share his sufferings, if we are to share his glory* (Rom. 8:14-17). Sanctifying grace, with the in-dwelling of the Holy Spirit in our soul, is the pledge of our participation in the victory of Christ over death, a victory that will last for all eternity in heaven.

In order to reject the Church's teaching on grace, it would logically be necessary to eliminate from Holy Scripture the Letter to the Romans as well as many passages from other Epistles.

Justification by faith, faith proved by deeds

> *All of us have a scrutiny to undergo before Christ's judgement seat, for each to reap what his mortal life has earned, good or ill, according to his deeds* (2 Cor. 5:10).

The Letter of St. Paul to the Romans is well known for its teaching on justification by faith. *Our contention is, that a man is justified by faith apart from the observances of the Law* (Rom. 3:28). From this to the conclusion that we can be saved without good deeds, there is only one step. However, the same inspired writer who said *When a man's faith is reckoned virtue in him, according to God's gracious plan, it is not because of anything he does; it is because he has faith, faith in the God who makes a just man of the sinner* (Rom. 4:5), also declares that God *will award to every man what his acts have deserved; eternal life to those who have striven for glory, and honour, and immortality, by persevering in doing good; the retribution of his anger to those who are contumacious, rebelling against the truth and paying homage to wickedness* (Rom. 2:6-8).

St. Paul was contrasting faith and the observances of mosaic law. He never intended to deny the necessity of good works; he was explaining the necessity of God's grace to perform acts of a supernatural value, and the fact that this grace is a totally free gift from God, granted to man through the infinite divine mercy.

This interpretation is confirmed by countless other statements to be found in Holy Scripture. A few examples will suffice. In the Book of Apocalypse we read: *I heard a voice, too, from heaven, Write thus: Blessed are the dead who die in the Lord. Yes, for ever henceforward, the Spirit says, they are to have rest from their labours; but the deeds they did in life go with them now* (Apoc. 14:13). Describing a vision of the Judgement, St. John writes: *And the dead were judged by their deeds, as the books recorded them* (Apoc. 20:12). This testimony is particularly forceful if we take into account God's warning: *if anyone cancels a word in this book of prophecy, God will cancel his share in the book of life, in the holy city, in all that this book promises* (Apoc. 22:19).

The Apostle James exhorts Christians to put into

practice the Faith they have learned, for Faith without Love is a dead Faith, and love without deeds is a lie. *Faith, if it has no deeds to show for itself, has lost its own principle of life. We shall be inclined to say to him, Thou hast faith, but I have deeds to show. Show me this faith of thine without any deeds to prove it, and I am prepared, by my deeds, to prove my own faith. Thou believest that there is only one God; that is well enough, but then, so do the devils, and the devils shrink from him in terror* (James 2:17-19). After all, since he was vanquished by the Saviour's Death and Resurrection, the devil firmly believes that Jesus Christ is the Son of God, the Redeemer of mankind; but this *faith* cannot save him because he is incapable of deeds of love. *How is it that you call me, Master, Master, and will not do what I bid you? If anyone comes to me and listens to my commandments and carries them out, I will tell you what he is like; he is like a man that would build a house, who dug, dug deep, and laid his foundation on rock. Then a flood came, and the river broke upon that house, but could not stir it; it was founded upon rock. But the man who listens to what I say and does not carry it out is like a man who built his house in the earth without foundation; when the river broke upon it, it fell at once, and great was that house's ruin* (Luke 6:46-49). St. James echoed this teaching of the Master when he wrote: *be patient, and cherish that word implanted in you which can bring salvation to your souls. Only you must be honest with yourselves; you are to live by the word, not content merely to listen to it* (James 1:21-22).

When describing the Last Judgement, Jesus makes us understand that He expects good deeds from us, and will punish not only evil deeds but also sins of omission. *And he will answer them, Believe me, when you refused it to one of the least of my brethren here, you refused it to me* (Matt. 25:45). St. James, inspired by the Holy Spirit, spoke clearly about man's obligation to perform good deeds: *Yes, if a man has the power to do good, it is sinful in him to leave it undone* (James 4:17). The Bible ends on a note of warning: *Patience, I am coming soon; and with me comes the award I make, repaying each man according to the life he has lived* (Apoc. 22:12). And again Christ offers us the living water, the gift of his grace: *Come, you who are thirsty, take, you who will, the water of life; it is my free gift* (Apoc. 22:17).

The tendency to sin remains

> *Why then, since we are watched from above by such a cloud of witnesses, let us rid ourselves of all that weighs us down, of the sinful habit that clings so closely, and run, with all endurance, the race for which we are entered* (Heb. 12:1).

In Baptism we were freed from sin in the sense that we were made capable of overcoming the snares of the devil, of controlling our passions and performing supernaturally good deeds. However, the consequences of sin continue to weigh us down and require struggle on the part of the Christian: an optimistic struggle, for the Christian knows that he can rely on God's help.

Each day, while the word 'today' has still a meaning, strengthen your own resolution, to make sure that none of you grows hardened; sin has such power to cheat us (Heb. 3:13). Indeed, the Epistles of the New Testament contain countless exhortations to an improvement of life, and words of rebuke with reference to weaknesses that were evident among members of Christian communities. *Do not these rivalries, these dissensions among you show that nature is still alive, that you are guided by human standards?* (1 Cor. 3:3), St. Paul points out. And St. James says: *What leads to war, what leads to quarrelling among you? I will tell you what leads to them; the appetites that infest your mortal bodies* (James 4:1).

The Christian continues being subjected to temptations, with a real danger of falling. Sometimes those temptations come directly from the devil: *Be sober and watch well; the devil, who is your enemy, goes about roaring like a lion, to find his prey, but you, grounded in the faith, must face him boldly* (1 Peter 5:8-9). Often, however, the devil does not need to tempt us, because we already have acquired bad habits and do not have the necessary determination to struggle: *Nobody, when he finds himself tempted, should say, I am being tempted by God. God may threaten us with evil, but he does not himself tempt anyone. No, when a man is tempted, it is always because he is being drawn away by the lure of his own passions. When that has come about, passion conceives and gives birth to sin; and when sin has reached its full growth, it breeds death* (James 1:12-15).

No-one can consider himself free from temptation. No-one is above temptation. And, as long as we are still journeying on this earth, we face the possibility of falling into sin. In his First Letter to the

Corinthians, St. Paul explains it by comparing the members of the Church to the sons of Israel. After urging his readers to struggle to be masters of themselves (cf. 1 Cor. 9:24-27), he explains how the passage of the Israelites through the Red Sea was a figure of Baptism, the manna a figure of the Bread of Life; so blessed by God, the Chosen People were expected to obey God's commandments, and yet they rebelled against God and were punished by Him. All this, St. Paul says, is to be a warning to God's People, the Church. *When all this happened to them, it was a symbol; the record of it was written as a warning to us, in whom history has reached its fulfilment; and it means that he who thinks he stands firmly should beware of a fall. I pray that no temptation may come upon you that is beyond man's strength* (1 Cor. 10:11-13).

No-one can say: I am already saved and cannot sin any longer. Who more than St. Paul could have boasted of having secured his own salvation? Yet he said: *Not that I have already won the prize, already reached fulfilment. I only press on, in the hope of winning the mastery, as Christ Jesus has won the mastery over me. No, brethren, I do not claim to have the mastery already, but this at least I do; forgetting what I have left behind, intent on what lies before me, I press on with the goal in view, eager for the prize, God's heavenly summons in Christ Jesus* (Phil. 3:12-14). He kept on the struggle: *I buffet my own body, and make it my slave; or I, who have preached to others, may myself be rejected* (1 Cor. 9:27).

One might object and ask: then, how can we say that Jesus Christ saved us from the devil and from sin, if we remain vulnerable and run constant risk of falling into sin?

This is God's plan of salvation already foreshadowed in the Old Testament. When God punished the rebellion of the Israelites by sending them fiery serpents, many people suffered snakebites and died. *Upon this, the Lord sent serpents among them, with fire in their fangs, that struck at many and killed many of them, till they came to Moses and confessed, We have sinned by making complaints against the Lord and against thee; entreat him to rid us of the serpents. So Moses made intercession for the people; and the Lord bade him fashion a serpent of bronze, and set it up on a staff, bringing life to all who should look towards it as they lay wounded. And so it proved; when Moses made a brazen serpent and set it up on a staff, the wounded men had but to look towards it, and they were healed* (Num. 21:6-9).

The bronze serpent was a prophetic figure of Christ on the Cross, and of the salvation He would carry out, as St. John himself interpreted it: *And this Son of Man must be lifted up, as the serpent was lifted up by Moses in the wilderness; so that those who believe in him may not perish, but have eternal life* (John 3:14-15). It is very interesting to note that the people of Israel asked God to save their lives by removing the snakes, but God answered their prayer by giving them a cure for the snakebites; the snakes remained and people continued being bitten. Yet their lives were saved if they looked at the bronze serpent set high on a pole.

This is indeed what Christ came to do. He did not conquer death by eliminating it, but by rising from the dead. He did not conquer sin by eliminating it, but by giving us the means to fight it successfully and to get up again, should we fall.

So we are sure to face temptation in our life. But we are also sure that, provided we do not leave God, God will not leave us. *Not that God will play you false; he will not allow you to be tempted beyond your powers. With the temptation itself, he will ordain the issue of it, and enable you to hold your own* (1 Cor. 10:13).

What we need to do is to remain close to God. *Draw your strength from the Lord, from that mastery which his power supplies. You must wear all the weapons of God's armoury, if you would find the strength to resist the cunning of the devil* (Eph. 6:10-11). We hear the same teaching from St. James: *Stand firm against the devil, and he will run away from you, come close to God, and he will come close to you* (James 4:7-8). This explains why St. John says that *the man who has been born of God, we may be sure, keeps clear of sin; that divine origin protects him, and the evil one cannot touch him* (1 John 5:18); St. John is not implying that a man who has received the new birth through water and the Holy Spirit is incapable of sinning, but only that, as long as he responds to God's grace, he will not sin.

Freedom of man and grace of God

Beloved, choose the right pattern, not the wrong, to imitate (3 John 11).

God's grace is powerful and effective. *With what*

grace God gives me (and he gives it in all the effectiveness of his power), I am a minister of that Gospel (Eph. 3:7). It can overcome any obstacle and makes man able to win any battle in his interior life; it is a participation in God's own strength: *And indeed, for fear that these surpassing revelations should make me proud, I was given a sting to distress my outward nature, an angel of Satan to rebuff me. Three times it made me entreat the Lord to rid me of it; but he told me: My grace is enough for thee; my strength finds its full scope in thy weakness. More than ever, then, I delight to boast of the weaknesses that humiliate me, so that the strength of Christ may enshrine itself in me. I am well content with those humiliations of mine, with the insults, the hardships, the persecutions, the times of difficulty I undergo for Christ: when I am weakest, then I am strongest of all* (2 Cor. 12:7-10).

On the other hand, God respects man's freedom, and therefore the Christian has the possibility of choosing between God's will and his own disorderly desires, of accepting or rejecting God's grace. This is why St. Paul exhorted the Corinthians: *And now, to further that work, we entreat you not to offer God's grace an ineffectual welcome* (2 Cor. 6:1).

To achieve sanctity, it is not enough to receive God's grace; man must cooperate with grace by making personal efforts. St. Paul explains how God called us to holiness by pouring upon us the abundance of His grace, which is a participation in the divine nature: *He has chosen us out, in Christ, before the foundation of the world, to be saints, to be blameless in his sight, for love of him; marking us out beforehand (so his will decreed) to be his adopted children through Jesus Christ. Thus he would manifest the splendour of that grace by which he has taken us into his favour in the person of his beloved Son. It is in him and through his blood that we enjoy redemption, the forgiveness of our sins. So rich is God's grace, that has overflowed upon us in a full stream of wisdom and discernment, to make known to us the hidden purpose of his will* (Eph. 1:4-9). On the other hand, St. Peter reminds us that, precisely because we share in the divine nature, we must make every effort on our part to practise virtues in accordance with our dignity as God's children: *Through him God has bestowed on us high and treasured promises; you are to share the divine nature, with the world's corruption, the world's passions, left behind. And you too have to contribute every effort on your own part, crowning your faith with virtue, and virtue with enlightenment, and enlightenment with continence, and continence with endurance, and endurance with holiness, and holiness with brotherly love, and brotherly love with charity. Such gifts, when they are yours in full measure, will make you quick and successful pupils, reaching ever closer knowledge of our Lord Jesus Christ* (2 Peter 1:4-8).

And so, the better we respond to grace, the more grace God will bestow upon us: *Grow up in grace and in the knowledge of our Lord and Saviour Jesus Christ* (2 Peter 3:18). But we always retain the capacity to resist God's grace or to lose it altogether, and this is why St. Paul exhorts us: *Do not distress God's Holy Spirit, whose seal you bear until the day of your redemption comes* (Eph. 4:30).

Different degrees of sin

> *Sin may be wrongdoing of any kind; not*
> *all sin is fatal* (1 John 5:17).

The Church has always taught that there are
different degrees of sin. Experience and common sense
also show us that not all wrongdoing is equally sinful:
for example, total apostasy is much worse than one
isolated abstention from a grave religious duty; an
angry word is different from a full-scale quarrel;
slapping someone is not as sinful as murdering him. If
the offence is small, friendship with God is not lost,
although God is displeased, and forgiveness can easily
be obtained; it is called venial sin. If the offence is
serious, the sinner loses the grace of God, i.e. his
participation in God's own life, the supernatural life of
his soul, and as a consequence he finds himself
excluded from heaven; this is mortal sin. Some mortal
sins, by their very nature, harden the soul of the sinner
in such a way that they also block the channels of
forgiveness, excluding the possibility of repentance and
confession of sins. This is why St. John, speaking of the
need to pray for souls in the state of sin, makes a
distinction between different types of mortal sins
according to the capacity for repentance which remains
in the soul: *If a man knows his brother to be guilty, yet
not of such sin as brings death with it, he should pray for
him; and, at his request, life will be granted to the other
who is sinning, yet not fatally. There is a sin which kills;
it is not over this that I bid him fall to prayer. Sin may be
wrong-doing of any kind; not all sin is fatal* (John 5:16-
17). The Evangelist is speaking in both cases of mortal

sin, for he says that life will be granted to the sinner, who must therefore have previously lost the life of grace. When he adds that he does not ask Christians to pray for people guilty of *a sin which kills*, he is referring to some heinous sins which are very seldom remitted because they seldom give way to repentance, e.g. wilful apostasy from the faith, or hatred of God.

We find in the New Testament several enumerations – that are not meant to be exhaustive – of mortal sins. At the beginning of this chapter, we already quoted what Jesus Christ said about the sins that make a man unclean (cf. Matt. 15:19-20) and the words of St. Paul to the Galatians about the sins that proceed from corrupt nature (cf. Gal. 5:16-25). On another occasion, the Apostle of the Gentiles warned Christians: *Yet you know well enough that wrongdoers will not inherit God's kingdom. Make no mistake about it; it is not the debauched, the idolaters, the adulterous, it is not the effeminate, the sinners against nature, the dishonest, the misers, the drunkards, the bitter of speech, the extortioners that will inherit the kingdom of God* (1 Cor. 6:9-10).

Mortal sin deserves the punishment of hell. *Who wins the victory? He shall have his share in this; I will be his God, and he shall be my son. But not the cowards, not those who refuse belief, not those whose lives are abominable; not the murderers, the fornicators, the sorcerers, the idolaters, not those who are false in any of their dealings. Their lot awaits them in the lake that burns with fire and brimstone, and it is the second death* (Apoc. 21:7-8). Mortal sin is the only true evil to be feared because of its dreadful consequences: *And there is no need to fear those who kill the body, but have no means of killing the soul; fear him more, who has the power to ruin body and soul in hell* (Matt. 10:28).

Venial sin deserves temporal punishment. Although it does not kill the life of grace in the soul, it weakens it and makes it more vulnerable to temptations. A Christian must attach importance to venial sins and struggle to avoid them for, if he does not struggle, he might eventually fall into mortal sin.

In his goodness, God permits us to undergo in this present life the temporal punishment due to our sins, in order to purify us from our bad habits and strengthen our will against temptations. *It is those I love that I correct and chasten; kindle thy generosity and repent* (Apoc. 3:19), God said to the Christians of Laodicea. And St. Paul tells us: *Let us purge ourselves clean from every defilement of flesh and of spirit, achieving the work of our sanctification in the fear of God* (2 Cor. 7:1-2).

Not all Christians will reach perfection in this life. St. Paul explained to the Corinthians how all Christians must necessarily build up their lives upon Christ as their foundation, but their works will have different value according to their rectitude of intention, their supernatural outlook and their love for God. Some will build with poorer materials than others, and as a result their lives will lack solidity. Because they have not rejected Christ through mortal sin, however, they will be saved through the purifying fire of Purgatory: *the foundation which has been laid is the only one which anybody can lay; I mean Jesus Christ. But on this foundation different men will build in gold, silver, precious stones, wood, grass, or straw, and each man's workmanship will be plainly seen. It is the day of the Lord that will disclose it, since that day is to reveal*

*itself in fire, and fire will test the quality of each man's
workmanship. He will receive a reward, if the building he
has added on stands firm; if it is burnt up, he will be the
loser; and yet he himself will be saved, though only as
men are saved by passing through fire* (1 Cor. 3:11-15).
The last words imply some penal suffering, and as St.
Paul connects it closely to the Judgement Day, it must
include the idea of a painful purification after death,
i.e. Purgatory.

This passage applies more immediately to the
value of the work of different teachers who are all
imparting knowledge of Christ, but in a more or less
truthful way. If their teachings were not sound, the
Apostle says, they could still save their souls, but would
lose their special reward and would have to undergo
some punishment. Every Christian is, in some
measure, a teacher to others, and so the doctrine on
Purgatory contained in this passage of the Bible is
clear: the soul who is free from mortal sin, but whose
works were not of adequate value, will have to pass
through the fire of Purgatory before being admitted in
Heaven.

Holy Scripture encourages us to pray for the dead.
*A holy and wholesome thought it is to pray for the dead,
for their guilt's undoing* (2 Mac.12:46), the sacred writer
comments after telling how Judas Machabee and his
army prayed for their companions who had died in
battle: *Each of the fallen was wearing, under his shirt,
some token carried away from the false gods of Jamnia.
Here was defiance of the Jewish law, and none doubted
it was the cause of their undoing; none but praised the
Lord for his just retribution, that had brought hidden
things to light; and so they fell to prayer, pleading that the*

sin might go unremembered (Mac. 12:40-42). This is because we can help the souls of the departed who have not yet entered Heaven but are still undergoing purification in Purgatory.

Christians must try to avoid the slightest deliberate venial sin if they want to reach the heights of holiness to which they are called. Deliberate venial sin causes great harm by preventing us from rising closer to God. *Whoever, then, sets aside one of these commandments, though it were the least, and teaches men to do the like, will be of least account in the kingdom of heaven; but the man who keeps them and teaches others to keep them will be accounted in the kingdom of God as the greatest* (Matt. 5:19). It is difficult, for *we are betrayed, all of us, into many faults* (James 3:2), but with the grace of God we can be victorious. *Let us come boldly, then, before the throne of grace, to meet with mercy, and win that grace which will help us in our needs* (Heb. 4:16).

The forgiveness of sins after Baptism

> *Once more Jesus said to them, Peace be upon you; I came upon an errand from my Father, and now I am sending you out in my turn. With that, he breathed on them, and said to them, Receive the Holy Spirit; when you forgive men's sins, they are forgiven, when you hold them bound, they are held bound* (John 20:21-23).

The judicial power of Bishops

Jesus came upon earth to bring divine forgiveness. *That is what the Son of Man has come for, to search out and to save what was lost* (Luke 19:10). In his turn He sent His Apostles on the same errand. He entrusted to His representatives on earth the administration of His Justice and Mercy. *If thy brother does thee wrong, go at once and tax him with it, as a private matter between thee and him; and so, if he will listen to thee, thou hast won thy brother. If he will not listen to thee, take with thee one or two more, that the whole matter may be certified by the voice of two or three witnesses. If he will not listen to them, then speak of it to the church; and if he will not even listen to the church, then count him all one with the heathen and the publicans. I promise you, all that you bind on earth shall be bound in heaven, and all that you loose on earth shall be loosed in heaven* (Matt. 18:15-18). Christ repeated this injunction after His Resurrection: *when you forgive men's sins, they are forgiven, when you hold them bound, they are held bound* (John 20:23).

The Apostles understood this teaching of Christ as conferring them a judicial power over the members of the Church. To them belonged the authority to judge sinners in the name of God, absolving them from their sins or refusing absolution, imposing penalties upon the sinner or releasing him from them.

St. Peter was the first to exercise this jurisdiction. Faced with the hypocritical behaviour of Ananias and Sapphira, he declared their guilt: *It is God, not man, thou hast defrauded* (Acts 5:4) and pronounced the sentence: *What is this conspiracy between you, to put the Spirit of the Lord to the test? Even now I hear at the door the footsteps of those who have been burying thy husband; they will carry thee out too* (Acts 5:9). This sentence was ratified and carried out by God Himself. *And all at once she fell at his feet and died; so that when the young men came in they found her a corpse, and carried her out to bury her with her husband* (Acts 5:10).

The Letters of St. Paul to the Corinthians also give us an example of the judicial authority of the Apostles and their successors over the Christians ruled by them. *In the letter I wrote to you, I told you to avoid the company of fornicators; not meaning everyone in the world around you who is debauched, or a miser, or an extortioner, or an idolater; to do that, you would have to cut yourselves off from the world altogether. No, my letter meant that if anyone who is counted among the brethren is debauched, or a miser, or an idolater, or bitter of speech, or a drunkard, or an extortioner, you must avoid his company; you must not even sit at table with him. Why should I claim jurisdiction over those who are without? No, it is for you to pass judgement within your own number, leaving God to judge those who are without. Banish, then, the offender from your company* (1 Cor. 5:9-13).

The man in question had publicly committed a very serious sin, without much reaction on the part of the Christian community. St. Paul took stern measures. *For myself, though I am not with you in person, I am with you in spirit; and, so present with you, I have already passed sentence on the man who has acted thus. Call an assembly, at which I will be present in spirit, with all the power of our Lord Jesus Christ, and so, in the name of our Lord Jesus Christ, hand over the person named to Satan, for the overthrow of his corrupt nature, so that his spirit may find salvation in the day of our Lord Jesus Christ* (1 Cor. 5:3-5).

Jesus came to forgive, not to condemn. And so His Apostles and their successors, when they must condemn, do so with the desire of bringing about the sinner's repentance, which is an indispensable condition for God's forgiveness. We see St. Paul lifting the ban against the repentant sinner: *This punishment inflicted on him by so many of you is punishment enough for the man I speak of, and now you must think rather of showing him indulgence and comforting him; you must not let him be overwhelmed by excess of grief. Let me entreat you, then, to give him assurance of your good will* (2 Cor. 2:6-88). As he had ordered the handing over of the sinner to Satan (i.e. excommunication from the Church), St. Paul revoked the sentence, granting pardon in the name of Christ to rescue the repentant sinner from Satan's clutches. *I myself, wherever I have shown indulgence, have done so in the person of Christ for your sakes, for fear that Satan should get the advantage over us; we know well enough how resourceful he is* (2 Cor. 2:10-11).

The canonical penalty was lifted. All that remained was to complete the effects of the sinner's repentance and confession of his sins by granting him absolution.

The Sacrament of Penance: confession of sins to the priest

It is supposed here that the sinner whom St. Paul welcomes back into the Church in 2 Cor. 2:5-11 is the same person as in 1 Cor. 5:1-8. It makes no difference, however, if the Apostle is referring to two distinct cases. The fact is that one notorious sinner had been excluded from the Church, had repented and was consequently re-admitted in the Church.

What must have happened? St. Paul was not present in Corinth when all this took place. We can safely assume that the excommunicated man soon understood the wrong he had done and publicly regularised his situation. There must be more to it, for St. Paul knew that the man was deeply grieved. The repentant sinner must therefore have gone to the elders of the Church in Corinth, who would be the equivalent of the auxiliary bishops of a diocese or the parish priests; he confessed his sin to them and asked for forgiveness. Because of the canonical punishment of excommunication imposed on the sinner, the elders of the Church did not grant absolution immediately but referred the case to the Apostle Paul. All this took time, of course. St. Paul, informed of the sinner's true repentance, lifted the excommunication and authorised the elders to absolve the man and admit him again to the acts of worship and the Sacraments of the Church.

So the Bible offers us an example of the practice of sacramental confession. The material details of the administration of this Sacrament have varied in the course of time. In the matter of Confession as in many other matters, the Lord laid down the fundamental principles and left His Church in charge of determining in detail how things should be done. We must obey the Church as we obey Christ Himself, for *he who listens to you listens to me; he who despises you despises me* (Luke 10:16).

Jesus had always taught His disciples to respect the lawful religious authorities. After curing a leper, He commanded him to submit to the ritual of purification: *Go and show yourself to the priest, he said, and bring an offering for thy cleansing, as Moses commanded, to make the truth known to them* (Luke 5:14). He had already performed the miracle, but He did not excuse the man from submitting to the external ritual required by the Law. In the same way God forgives sins if and whenever He wants; He wants us, however, to perform the external acts established by Him for the forgiveness of sins: confession of our sins to the priest as an expression of a contrite heart.

Jesus had authority to forgive sins, and He entrusted it to the Apostles. *When you forgive men's sins, they are forgiven, when you hold them bound, they are held bound* (John 20:23). So if I sin gravely and confess my sin to God alone, God will withhold His pardon for I am refusing to pass through His appointed representative. Unless an Apostle forgives me, I shall not be forgiven. If I cannot find a priest to hear my confession, God will see my good will and will grant His forgiveness, for He remains the Supreme Judge; but I am still bound to go to confession at the first opportunity. If I refuse to confess my sin to a priest, my repentance is not authentic for I am still led by pride, unwilling to humble myself to obey God's command; my self-love – my vanity – is stronger than my love for God, and my sin cannot be forgiven.

The words of Jesus to the Apostles imply the obligation on the part of the sinner to go and tell his sins to the priest. If the priest is authorised to grant or to deny forgiveness, it must be because he has been told the circumstances of the sin. He is then able to judge whether or not there is effective repentance, and therefore whether or not absolution can be granted. Some sins remain inside the heart, such as lustful desires, thoughts of hatred, desires for revenge. Only God and the sinner know about those hidden sins. Yet the priest is the one who is to grant forgiveness in the name of God, and he can do so only if the sinner confesses his sin to him.

All sins, however great, can be forgiven

The Bible is full of calls to repentance. *As I live, saith the Lord God, I desire not the death of the wicked, but that the wicked turn from his way, and live. Turn ye, turn ye from your evil ways: and why will you die, O house of Israel?* (Ez. 33:11). God is a forgiving God, as Our Lord illustrated it in many parables such as the Lost Sheep (cf. Luke 15:1-7) and the Prodigal Son (cf. Luke 15:11-32).

Yet some passages seem to set a limit to God's mercy. Jesus had said: *And now I tell you this; there is pardon for all the other sins and blasphemies of men, but not for blasphemy against the Holy Spirit. There is no one who blasphemes against the Son of Man but may find forgiveness; but for him who blasphemes against the Holy Spirit there is no forgiveness, either in this world or in the world to come* (Matt. 12:31-32).

This passage must be understood in the light of all other teachings of Jesus Christ. The only limit to God's willingness to forgive is the freedom of man. The Prodigal Son was forgiven because he returned to his Father's house. The good thief was promised heaven because he humbly acknowledged his own sinfulness and asked for God's mercy, while the other shut himself off from the grace of God. Christ does not demand from us anything which He Himself is unwilling to do, and He commanded us: *as for thy brother, if he is at fault, tax him with it, and if he is sorry for it, forgive him; nay, if he does thee wrong seven times in the day, and seven times in the day comes back to thee and says, I am sorry, thou shalt forgive him* (Luke 17:3-4). So, provided there is repentance, God will not refuse His forgiveness. But what is repentance? It is what St. Paul calls supernatural remorse. He says: *supernatural remorse leads to an abiding and salutary change of heart* (2 Cor. 7:10). The sins against the Holy Spirit of which the Lord spoke must be sins that make such salutary change of heart extremely unlikely, e.g. stubbornness in sin, final impenitence, rejection of the known truth, apostasy. This interpretation is confirmed by other passages of the New Testament.

Thinking of persistent sinners, St. Paul says: *If we go on sinning wilfully, when once the full knowledge of the truth has been granted to us, we have no further sacrifice for sin to look forward to; nothing but a terrible expectation of judgement, a fire that will eagerly consume the rebellious* (Heb. 10:26-27). The reason is clear: the man who consciously rejects grace cannot ask God for mercy. *Let a man be convicted by two or three witnesses of defying the law of Moses and he dies, without hope of mercy. What of the man who has trampled the Son of God under foot, who has reckoned the blood of the covenant, that blood which sanctified him, as a thing unclean, mocked at the Spirit that brought him grace? Will not he incur a punishment much more severe?* (Heb. 10:28-29)

Speaking of Christians who denied Christ and returned to their pagan practices he affirms: *We can do nothing for those who have received, once for all, their enlightenment, who have tasted the heavenly gift, partaken of the Holy Spirit, known, too, God's word of comfort, and the powers that belong to a future life, and then fallen away. They cannot attain repentance through a second renewal. Would they crucify the Son of God a second time, hold him up to mockery a second time, for their own ends? No, a piece of ground which has drunk in, again and again, the showers which fell upon it, has God's blessing on it, if it yields a crop answering the needs of those who tilled it; if it bears thorns and thistles, it has lost its value; a curse hangs over it, and it will feed the bonfire at last* (Heb. 6:4-8). These are harsh words. They are not to be taken, however, as a refusal on the part of God to forgive; they rather describe a situation in which a man, baptised and confirmed, who has received in Holy Communion the Body and Blood of the Lord and has developed a certain intimacy with God, decides to turn away from Him and leaves the Church. Such a man is not likely to wish to return to God's Church. Yet God's mercy is infinite, and the repentant sinner is sure to be welcomed: *if your sins be as scarlet, they shall be made as white as snow: and if they be red as crimson, they shall be white as wool* (Is. 1:18). We can be sure that Christ continues seeking the conversion of the sinner, who will find forgiveness if he eventually turns to the Saviour: *Little children, the purpose of this letter is to keep you clear of sin. Meanwhile, if any of us falls into sin, we have an advocate to plead our cause before the Father in the Just One, Jesus Christ. He, in his own person, is the atonement made for our sins, and not only for ours, but for the sins of the whole world* (1 John 2:1-2).

The continuous need for penance — the value of suffering

> *Let us fix our eyes on Jesus, the origin and the crown of all faith, who, to win his prize of blessedness, endured the cross and made light of its shame, Jesus, who now sits on the right of God's throne. Take your standard from him, from his endurance, from the enmity the wicked bore him, and you will not grow faint, you will not find your souls unmanned* (Heb. 12:2-3).

We are all sinners, for we all have sinned. *Sin is with us; if we deny that, we are cheating ourselves; it means that truth does not dwell in us. No, it is when we confess our sins that he forgives our sins, ever true to his word, ever dealing right with us, and all our wrongdoing is purged away. If we deny that we have sinned, it means that we are treating him as a liar; it means that his word does not dwell in our hearts* (1 John 1:8-10). So we all must humble ourselves before God, first of all by turning to His mercy in the Sacrament of Penance, asking forgiveness for the sins we committed after Baptism, then performing acts of penance that will deaden our sinful passions, correct our bad habits and make us grow in the practice of virtue. *You must deaden, then, those passions in you which belong to earth, fornication and impurity, lust and evil desires, and that love of money which is idolatry. These are what brings down God's vengeance on the unbelievers, and such was our own behaviour, too, while you lived among*

*them. Now it is your turn to have done with it all,
resentment, anger, spite, insults, foul-mouthed utterance;
and do not tell lies at one another's expense. You must
be quit of the old self, and the habits that went with it;
you must be clothed in the new self, that is being refitted
all the time for closer knowledge, so that the image of
God who created it is its pattern* (Col. 3:4-10). We need
penance to reproduce in our life the life of Christ.

So, like St. Paul, we must practise voluntary
mortification: *I buffet my own body and make it my
slave* (1 Cor. 9:27). At the same time we must make
good use of the passive mortifications, i.e. the
difficulties and sufferings that come our way.

We should not be afraid of suffering. We must not
see suffering as a curse from God nor as an attack of
the devil upon us. *The branch that does yield fruit, he
trims clean, so that it may yield more fruit* (John 15:2),
and such trimming is painful. If we have the grace of
God in our soul and seek to do God's will, we shall see
in suffering a manifestation of the love of God who
wishes to correct our faults and make us grow in
holiness. *What if you have trials of many sorts to sadden
your hearts in this brief interval? That must needs
happen, so that you may give proof of your faith, a much
more precious thing than the gold we test by fire; proof
which will bring you praise, and glory, and honour when
Jesus Christ is revealed* (1 Peter 1:6-7). The Lord had
announced the necessity of suffering in the life of a
Christian: *He is not worthy of me, that does not take up
his cross and follow me* (Matt. 10:38).

The Letter to the Hebrews contains a beautiful
passage on the fruitfulness of suffering sent to us by
God to correct our errors. God's corrections enable us

to receive more grace and to purify ourselves here on earth. *My son, do not undervalue the correction which the Lord sends thee, do not be unmanned when he reproves thy faults. It is where he loves that he bestows correction; there is no recognition for any child of his, without chastisement. Be patient, then, while correction lasts; God is treating you as his children. Was there ever a son whom his Father did not correct? No, correction is the common lot of all; you must be bastards, not true sons, if you are left without it. We have known what it was to accept correction from earthly fathers, and with reverence; shall we not submit, far more willingly, to the Father of a world of spirits, and draw life from him? They, after all, only corrected us for a short while, at their own caprice; he does it for our good, to give us a share in that holiness which is his. For the time being, all correction is painful rather than pleasant; but afterwards, when it has done its work of discipline, it yields a harvest of good disposition, to our great peace. Come then, stiffen the sinews of drooping hand, and flagging knee, and plant your footprints in a straight track, so that the man who goes lame may not stumble out of the path, but regain strength instead* (Heb. 12:5-13).

We shall never have finished with doing penance, for even when we have purified ourselves of all remnants of sin, we are still called to do penance, as Christ did, for the sins of others. *Indeed you are engaged to this by the call of Christ; he suffered for our sakes, and left you his own example; you were to follow in his footsteps* (1 Peter 2:21).

Such a teaching is not a source of sadness. Indeed, Christianity is a religion full of joy. Love is as inseparable from suffering as it is from joy. The Acts tell us how the Apostles *left the presence of the Council, rejoicing that they had been found worthy to suffer indignity for the sake of Jesus' name* (Acts 5:41). This joy has never left the true disciples of Christ generation after generation. Like St. Paul we also can say: *I am glad of my sufferings on your behalf, as, in this mortal frame of mine, I help to pay off the debt which the afflictions of Christ still leave to be paid, for the sake of his body, the Church* (Col. 1:24).

The early Christians and the Sacrament of Penance or Confession

We have seen what the Bible itself tells us about the confession of sins. Now we can consider the testimony of history to see how the immediate successors of the Apostles and the whole Christian people understood the teaching of Christ on the forgiveness of sins committed after Baptism.

The *Didache* or *Instruction of the Lord to the Gentiles by means of the Twelve Apostles*, written as early as between 80 and 100 A.D. (i.e. before some books of the New Testament), states that a Christian must confess his sins before receiving Holy Communion. One century later a great Christian Apologist, Tertullian, wrote on the need for Confession for the remission of sins.

Nowadays, some people object to the teaching of the Church on Confession, claiming that it is sufficient to confess directly to God. There were very different objections in the first three centuries of Christianity: some were so strict as to consider that certain sins were unforgivable, so that God, and therefore also the

Church, could never pardon them.

It is extremely interesting to observe why the practice of Confession was very restricted in the first few centuries of the Christian era. No-one contested the need for the Sacrament of Penance to obtain the forgiveness of sins; on the contrary, Christians took a very stern stand. It was considered that a Christian had received such extraordinary graces from God in Baptism, Confirmation and Holy Communion that he was without excuse if he fell back into serious sin; therefore many representatives of the Church were ready to grant God's pardon only once in a lifetime. A repentant sinner was expected to do rigorous penance over a long period of time, and in many cases the absolution was granted only on his death bed. Indeed, if the early Christians seldom went to Confession, it was certainly not with the idea that God forgave their sins without the intervention of His priests. They knew that they remained in mortal sin and deserved the pains of hell until a representative of Christ granted them God's pardon.

It is also interesting to note that the Bishop of Rome, the Pope, granted forgiveness more easily than others in spite of the opposition of some who considered him excessively lenient.

Such rigour made Confession difficult. Because they remained in their sins, more and more people never received Holy Communion. The Church saw the need for a greater recourse to God's mercy. It was not easy to overcome the passivity of so many members of the Church who had become lukewarm. Finally, in the year 1215, the Fourth Lateran Council convoked by Pope Innocent III imposed upon all Christians the obligation of confessing their mortal sins and receiving Holy Communion at least once a year. The Good Shepherd was taking steps to ensure that Christians would not remain cut off from God's grace for the greatest part of their lives.

From this brief survey of the faith of the Christian people throughout the first 1200 years of our era, one can see that the need for Confession to obtain forgiveness was always firmly believed in, because it was an integral part of the deposit of Faith. Only with the rise of Protestantism in the 16th century was this Sacrament contested. But the Protestant idea of confessing sins to God alone and not to His representatives on earth is in opposition to the teachings of Christ and to the Faith of the first Christians. It does not have its roots in the Bible or in the practice of the early Church.

7

The Domestic Church
The Sacrament of Matrimony

> *That is why a man will leave his father and mother and will cling to his wife, and the two will become one flesh. Yes, those words are a high mystery, and I am applying them here to Christ and his Church. Meanwhile each of you is to love his wife as he would love himself, and the wife is to pay reverence to her husband* (Eph. 5:31-33).

Marriage, a divine vocation

> *So God made man in his own image and likeness, made him in the image of God. Man and woman both, he created them. And God pronounced his blessing on them, Increase and multiply and fill the earth, and make it yours* (Gen. 1:27-28).

God Himself, in the beginning, made man and woman and gave them a share in His creative power. One man and one woman were entrusted by God with the task of filling the earth and subduing it. The Bible gives us, in a few brief sentences, a picture of marriage as an institution of divine origin, not only tolerated but positively willed by God as the source of the fundamental constitutive element of society: the family. One man and one woman were to become one flesh, and from their union other lives would spring; together, husband and wife would work to build up society. They would educate their children and prepare them to assume their own responsibilities.

God created man for eternal life, for holiness. Marriage was part of God's plan for man well before original sin upset the order established by the Creator. Therefore marriage is a true vocation: the path to holiness marked out by God for the majority of men and women. In the course of time, the thorns and thistles of sin invaded this path and made it difficult to follow, until Jesus Christ restored it to its original purity.

In order to save mankind, God chose to be born in the heart of a family; from a virgin mother but, all the same, within a family which nothing external differentiated from any other family. Christ attended the wedding feast of Cana and worked His first miracle for the benefit of the bride and bridegroom (cf. John 2:1-11). In the parable of the Great Supper Christ taught that marriage cannot be taken as an excuse to neglect God's call to holiness (cf. Luke 14:16-24). Years later St. Paul would remind Christians: *Marriage, in every way, must be held in honour, and the marriage-bed kept free from stain. Over fornication and adultery, God will call us to account* (Heb. 13:4).

Because Marriage is holy, it requires a preparation, a training in holiness, for husband and wife to live up to their vocation. Because it involves a complete self-giving, each person has to guard his or her own body and heart, to preserve its integrity, so that it can be offered to the spouse as an unspoiled gift of lasting value. In one word, they must come to understand the true meaning of love.

Christian love and holy purity

What God asks of you is that you should sanctify yourselves, and keep clear of fornication. Each of you must learn to control his own body, as something holy and held in honour, not yielding to the promptings of passion, as the heathen do in their ignorance of God. None of you is to be exorbitant, and take advantage of his brother, in his business dealings. For all such wrong-doing God exacts punishment; we have told you so already, in solemn warning. The life to which God has called us is not one of incontinence, it is a life of holiness, and to despise it is to despise, not man, but God, the God who has implanted his Holy Spirit in us. As for love of the brethren, there is no need to send you any message; you have learned for yourselves God's lesson about the

> *charity we ought to show to one another*
> (1 Thess. 4:3-9).

The Christian religion is essentially a religion of Love. *The mark by which all men will know you for my disciples will be the love you bear one another* (John 13:35), the Lord said. Unfortunately, the word *love* is frequently misunderstood and has acquired, in modern times, sensual connotations totally foreign to its true meaning. Jesus gave us a model of perfect Christian love: *I have a new commandment to give you, that you are to love one another; that your love for one another is to be like the love I have borne you* (John 13:34).

Jesus' love for us had nothing to do with sensual pleasure or with sentimentalism. *This is my commandment, that you should love one another, as I have loved you. This is the greatest love a man can show, that he should lay down his life for his friends* (John 15:12-13). His love was expressed in sacrifice, in suffering, in constant self-denial that culminated in His Passion and Death on the Cross. And such our love must be.

There are only three types of loves offered for our consideration in the Bible: the love between parents and children (paternal/maternal and filial love), between husband and wife (conjugal love) and between brothers and sisters (fraternal love). Love between friends is assimilated to fraternal love, for we are all children of God. There is no room for sensuality between brothers and sisters, and so the love that may grow between a man and a woman not yet joined in wedlock must be a chaste love, *not yielding to the promptings of passion, as the heathens do in their ignorance of God* (1 Thess. 4:5). To act otherwise is to follow pagan ways, by committing fornication.

The dictionary defines fornication as 'sexual intercourse outside marriage'. The Christian teaching on this is clear: *None of you must be guilty of fornication* (Heb. 12:16); instead, *let brotherly love be firmly established among you* (Heb. 13:1).

Continence is not only possible, but necessary for unmarried people. True, the body has needs that claim satisfaction. But we must distinguish between real needs and disorderly inclinations. Food is necessary for every individual in order to keep alive. Sexual intercourse, by contrast, is only necessary for the survival of the species, but not for the life of each individual, and it must be exercised according to God's laws, i.e. within marriage.

I am free to do what I will, but I must not abdicate my own liberty (1 Cor. 6:12), St. Paul explained to the Corinthians, fearing that his Gentile readers, aware of their freedom from the ceremonial obligations of the Jewish law, might consider themselves dispensed from its moral obligations as well. *Food is meant for our animal nature, and our animal nature claims its food; true enough, but then, God will bring both one and the other to an end. But your bodies are not meant for debauchery, they are meant for the Lord, and the Lord claims your bodies. And God, just as he has raised our Lord from the dead, by his great power will raise us up too. Have you never been told that your bodies belong to the body of Christ? And am I to take what belongs to Christ and make it one with a harlot? God forbid. Or did you never hear that the man who unites himself to a harlot becomes one body with her? The two, we are told, will become one flesh. Whereas the man who unites himself to the Lord becomes one spirit with him. Keep clear, then, of debauchery. Any other sin a man commits, leaves the body untouched, but the fornicator is committing a crime against his own body* (1 Cor. 6:12-18).

God dwells in our bodies, through grace, as in a Temple: *Surely, you know that your bodies are the shrines of the Holy Spirit, who dwells in you. And he is God's gift to you, so that you are no longer your own masters. A great price was paid to ransom you; glorify God by making your bodies the shrines of his presence* (1 Cor. 6:19-20).

The Letter of St. Paul to the Ephesians contains abundant teaching on Christian love and on Marriage. *May your lives be rooted in love, founded on love. May you and all the saints be enabled to measure, in all its breadth and length and height and depth, the love of Christ, to know what passes knowledge* (Eph. 3:17-19). A Christian must follow Christ's example of love.

As God's favoured children, you must be like him. Order your lives in charity, upon the model of that charity which Christ showed to us, when he gave himself up on our behalf, a sacrifice breathing out fragrance as he offered it to God. As for debauchery, and impurity of every kind, and covetousness, there must be no whisper of it among you; it would ill become saints (Eph. 5:1-3).

Thou shalt not covet thy neighbour's wife. Indeed, holy purity concerns not only the body, but the heart. If we do not guard our heart, it will lose its power to love because we have wasted this God-given power, opening the door to the defilement of sinful desires. *You have heard that it was said, Thou shalt not commit adultery.*

*But I tell you that he who casts his eyes on a woman so
as to lust after her has already committed adultery with
her in his heart* (Matt. 5:27-28). Unguarded senses open
the way to lust, lust leads to fornication, and fornication
excludes one from the Kingdom of Heaven.

When two young people are thinking of marriage,
they must lay the foundation of their future conjugal
life upon holy purity. Like the man who sat down to
calculate his costs before building a tower (cf. Luke
14:28-30), they need some time to get to know each
other in depth, to discover each other's personality and
character, qualities and defects, ambitions and fears.
Indeed they must find out whether they really want to
spend a lifetime together, whether their mutual
dealings are sufficiently rich in content to enable them
continue to be happy in each other's company after the
first fire of their honeymoon. If their love passes this
test, the time has come to commit themselves to each
other before God. Then their union is something really
precious: not a conditional or temporary association,
but a complete gift of self, body and spirit. It is a
permanent, irrevocable and fruitful partnership of love.

The Bible compares married love to the love that
exists between Christ and His Church. *You who are
husbands must show love to your wives, as Christ
showed love to the Church when he gave himself up on
its behalf ...; he would summon it into his own
presence, the Church in all its beauty, no stain, no
wrinkle, no such disfigurement* (Eph. 5:25-27). This
evokes a virginal love, the love of a pure heart.

The Gospels give us a striking example of chaste
love. No man has ever been more in love than St.
Joseph. It was precisely because he loved Mary so

much that he agreed to preserve her virginity. He knew
the ideal God had inspired in her, and he respected it.
He did not look upon her as an object to be possessed,
but as a wonderful person for whom it was worthwhile
to live. Any sacrifice would be a small price, he
thought, for the privilege of spending his life near her
and being the instrument of her happiness.

It is not an impossible task for an engaged couple
to safeguard their purity, for Christ gave us the means
to do so. First of all, prayer: *Watch and pray, that you
may not enter into temptation* (Matt. 26:41). Then,
guard of the senses, to avoid occasions of sin: *If thy
hand is an occasion of falling to thee, cut it off; better for
thee to enter into life maimed, than to have two hands
when thou goest into hell, into unquenchable fire; the
worm which eats them there never dies, the fire is never
quenched. And if thy foot is an occasion of falling to
thee, cut it off; better for thee to enter into eternal life
lame, than to have both feet when thou art cast into the
unquenchable fire of hell; the worm which eats them
there never dies, the fire is never quenched. And if thy eye
is an occasion of falling, pluck it out; better for thee to
enter blind into the kingdom of God, than to have two
eyes when thou art cast into the fire of hell* (Mark 9:42-
46). The Lord is evidently not recommending self-
mutilation: He asks us to renounce watching anything
that will constitute for us an incitement to sin, listening
to invitations to sin, or going where we are likely to be
induced to sin.

Thus God has given us some warnings similar to
the danger signals of the Highway Code. These are not
intended to limit our freedom but to help us exercise it
by enabling us to reach our goal faster. To love consists

in seeking the highest good of the beloved. True love goes together with respect, delicacy of feelings, refinement of manners in mutual dealings. A man in love seeks ways of being of service to his beloved and making her happy. Such a generous love is forged in the course of a chaste courtship.

We should seek strength for our purity in Holy Communion, for *he who eats my flesh and drinks my blood, lives continually in me, and I in him* (John 6:57), asking for and receiving forgiveness and the help of grace in the Sacrament of Penance as often as necessary.

The concept of love includes faithfulness. Faithfulness presupposes commitment. The union between a man and a woman does not deserve to be called love unless it is the consequence of a permanent and exclusive commitment acquired before God, and that is Christian Marriage.

Unity and indissolubility of marriage

> *If a man puts away his wife and marries another, he behaves adulterously towards her, and if a woman puts away her husband and married another, she is an adulteress* (Mark 10:11-12)

Thou shalt not commit adultery, God tells us. Jesus Christ explained to us the full implications of this commandment. He directly condemned the practice of divorce and remarriage, thereby also condemning polygamy: if it is sinful to take a second wife after separating from the first, it is just as sinful to maintain two wives at the same time.

One may feel tempted to do like the Jews and say: the patriarchs practised polygamy and divorce was allowed under the mosaic law, so it cannot have been sinful. The Lord's answer is valid for both practices: *It was to suit your hard hearts that Moses allowed you to put your wives away; it was not so at the beginning of things* (Matt. 19:8).

Nowhere in the Bible is there a positive approval of polygamy and divorce. These were practices tolerated by God in His great patience and understanding of the weakness of human nature deprived of sanctifying grace. But Christ came to reconcile men with God, to make them participate in the divine life; now every Christian, born to a new life through water and the Holy Spirit, must follow *the model of that charity which Christ showed to us when he gave himself up on our behalf, a sacrifice breathing out fragrance as he offered it to God* (Eph. 5:2). Husband and wife must take as their model the love that binds Christ and the Church. Christ founded only One Church, and His love is faithful. The Church cannot follow any other leader but Christ who speaks and acts through His chosen representatives. The unity and indissolubility of marriage is a reflection of the Lord's perpetual and loving presence in the One True Church.

Christ restored Marriage to its original purity. Man and woman are equal in dignity. Adam recognised in Eve the same nature as his own: *Here, at last, is bone that comes from mine, flesh that comes from mine; it shall be called Woman, this thing that was taken out of*

Man (Gen. 2:23). The sacred writer affirms from that moment the indissolubility of marriage: *so that the two become one flesh*, for one flesh cannot be divided. Christ pointed out the fact that marriage is between one man and one woman only when he referred to this passage of Genesis and added: *therefore now they are not two but one flesh* (Matt. 19:6).

St. Paul reiterated the Lord's precept of faithfulness between husband and wife. *For those who have married already, the precept holds which is the Lord's precept, not mine; the wife is not to leave her husband (if she has left him, she must either remain unmarried, or go back to her own husband again), and the husband is not to put away his wife* (1 Cor. 7:10-11). Husband and wife have the duty to live together, forming a stable family.

There are some cases in which separation is acceptable, e.g. the unfaithfulness of one of the spouses. This is the meaning of the apparent exception made by the Lord to the prohibition of divorce as St. Matthew recorded in his gospel: *And I tell you that he who puts away his wife, not for any unfaithfulness of hers, and so marries another, commits adultery;* and he too commits adultery, who marries her after she has been put away* (Matt. 19:9). The infidelity of one of the

---

* The text of the Douay-Rheims version of the Gospel says: *And I say to you, that whosoever shall put away his wife, except it be for fornication, and shall marry another, committeth adultery*. This translation follows more closely the Greek and Latin texts and is in better agreement with Matt. 5:32.

spouses is a lawful cause for separation, for God does not impose the obligation to live with a faithless spouse, but it never justifies marrying again.

Jesus had already spoken about this earlier on in His ministry. *But I tell you that the man who puts away his wife (setting aside the matter of unfaithfulness) makes an adulteress of her, and whoever marries her after she has been put away, commits adultery* (Matt. 5:32). The unfaithful wife was already an adulteress; therefore, by sending her away the injured husband was not inciting her to commit adultery. But even if separation is justified by some serious motive, the marriage bond remains in full force and no second marriage is possible.

Only the death of one of the spouses can put an end to marriage. *As for a wife, she is yoked to her husband as long as she lives; if her husband is dead, she is free to marry anyone she will, so long as she marries in the Lord* (1 Cor. 7:39).

The purpose of marriage

And God pronounced his blessing on them, Increase and multiply and fill the earth (Gen. 1:28).

We must turn to the Old Testament for a clear statement on the purpose of marriage. It was so evident to all in Jesus' times that He only confirmed the divine institution of Marriage as it had been willed by the Creator. *Have you never read, how he who created them, when they first came to be, created them male and female; and how he said, A man, therefore, will leave his father and mother and will cling to his wife, and the two will become one flesh; what God, then, has joined, let no man put asunder* (Matt. 19:4-6).

The first purpose stated in the Bible is the procreation of children: *Increase and multiply* (Gen. 1:28). We are also told of another purpose, that of mutual help and companionship, coming first in chronological order but not in importance: *It is not well that man should be without companionship; I will give him a mate of his own kind* (Gen. 2:18).

Procreation of children and mutual help: these explain why God wanted the unity and indissolubility of Marriage. There is no mutual help if husband and wife can abandon each other at will. In addition, children are to be brought up, educated, cared for during many years, and this cannot be achieved satisfactorily without the stability of a permanent home and the loving attention of a father and a mother.

Holy Scripture is full of statements in praise of large families, and children are invariably seen as a blessing, as a source of joy and holy pride. *Lo, sons are a heritage from the Lord, the fruit of the womb a reward* (Ps. 127:3). *Your wife will be like a fruitful vine within your house; your children will be like olive shoots around your table. Lo, thus shall the man be blessed who fears the Lord* (Ps. 128:3, 4).

Putting obstacles to the procreation of children means going against God's purpose for Marriage. It is therefore a sin. In spite of its antiquity, the Bible has something to teach modern man on the sinfulness of contraceptives. Evidently, we shall not find in it a direct reference to artificial methods of birth control, for the men and women of biblical times always longed to perpetuate themselves in their children, and they rightly considered children as a blessing from God. But Holy Scripture lays down a principle which can easily be applied to each practical situation: it is gravely sinful to frustrate the marriage act, i.e. to perform it in such a way as to ensure that no new life can spring from it, putting means to obstruct natural intercourse.

We read about this in the Book of Genesis. A woman called Tamar was married to Er, son of Juda. *This first-born son of his was a sinner, and God saw it and cut him off in his prime* (Gen. 38:7). Er died without children. According to the customs of those days Onan, brother of the dead man, was expected to take the widow and beget children in his brother's name. *Whereupon Juda bade his son Onan mate with the widow, and do a husband's duty by her, so as to beget children in his brother's name; but Onan, who knew that they would not be reckoned as his, frustrated the act of marriage when he mated with her, sooner than breed sons in his brother's name. Him, too, for this abominable deed of his, the Lord punished with death* (Gen. 38:8-10).

This sin which God punished with death is still called, to this day, onanism. And it is just as sinful today as it was in the time of the patriarchs, for Christ said: *Do not think that I have come to set aside the Law and the prophets; I have not come to set them aside, but to bring them to perfection* (Matt. 5:17).

Onanism and any artificial contraceptive methods are a manifestation of selfishness and are motivated by lust, not by love, for love tends to be fruitful. Married people would do well to make their own the prayer which young Tobias and Sara addressed to God on their wedding night: *Lord God of our fathers, Tobias said, praise be to thee from heaven and earth, from seas and fountains and rivers, and from all creatures of thine that make in these their homes! When Adam was made of earth's clay, it was by thy hand; when Eve was sent to cheer him, it was of thy gift. Thou, Lord, art my witness that I wed this sister of mine not from love of dalliance; only in the dear hope of leaving a race behind me, a race in whose destiny, Lord, may thy name be ever blessed! And thus Sara prayed, Have mercy on us, Lord, have mercy on us; safe from all harm grow we old together, he and I!* (Tob. 8:7-10).

This love between husband and wife enables them to live together with a generous spirit and a chaste heart, each spouse seeking first of all the happiness of the other. We find in Zachary a good model of conjugal love. From what the Gospel tells us (Luke 1:1-25), it appears that he had remained faithful to his wife Elizabeth in spite of their having no children. This shows the depth of his affection for her, because the Jews considered childlessness a powerful reason for marrying again. The love of Zachary and Elizabeth was strong enough to overcome this difficulty: it was just as fresh in their old age as on their wedding day.

The married man does not belong to himself any longer: he belongs to his wife, just as his wife belongs to him. Each spouse should think of duties rather than of rights; then there is no room for rancour and self-pity. *Let every man give his wife what is her due, and every woman do the same by her husband; he, not she, claims the right over her body, as she, not he, claims the right over his. Do not starve one another, unless perhaps*

*you do so for a time, by mutual consent, to have more
freedom for prayer; come together again, or Satan will
tempt you, weak as you are* (1 Cor. 7:3-5).

This is a demanding ideal, a true call from God, a
vocation to sanctity. Human nature is weak, and
Christians need the help of God's grace to live up to
the demands of Marriage, to be able to love each other
as Christ loves His Church. They receive that grace in
the Sacrament of Matrimony.

The sacrament of Matrimony

> *That is why a man will leave his father
> and mother and will cling to his wife, and
> the two will become one flesh. Yes, those
> words are a high mystery, and I am
> applying them here to Christ and his
> Church* (Eph. 5:31-32).

In his Epistle to the Ephesians, St. Paul describes
the unique character of the conjugal union.

First he explains that, as there is an order in
society, there is an order in the family, which is the
smallest and most important unit of society. Social
order requires an authority. And so God placed the
man as head of the family. Authority, however, is not to
be understood as tyranny; on the contrary, it is a loving
service for the benefit of the community. Therefore
there is no room for oppression and fear in the
relationship between husband and wife. The spouses
must love each other with the love of Christ.

Wives must obey their husbands as they would obey

the Lord. The man is the head to which the woman's body is united, just as Christ is the head of the Church, he, the Saviour on whom the safety of his body depends; and women must owe obedience at all points to their husbands, as the Church does to Christ. You who are husbands must show love to your wives, as Christ showed love to the Church when he gave himself up on its behalf. He would hallow it, purify it by bathing it in the water to which his word gave life; he would summon it into his own presence, the Church in all its beauty, no stain, no wrinkle, no such disfigurement; it was to be holy, it was to be spotless. And that is how husband ought to love wife, as if she were his own body; in loving his wife, a man is but loving himself. It is unheard of, that a man should bear ill-will to his own flesh and blood; no, he keeps it fed and warmed; and so it is with Christ and his Church; we are limbs of his body; flesh and bone, we belong to him. That is why a man will leave his father and mother and will cling to his wife, and the two will become one flesh. Yes, those words are a high mystery, and I am applying them here to Christ and his Church (Eph. 5:22-32).

The Greek word for *mystery* – μυστηριον – could also be translated as *sacrament*, meaning *sign of something hidden*. Indeed, Holy Scripture tells us that God wanted to establish Marriage as a visible sign of something hidden to the eyes: the love of the spouses must be an image of the love between Christ and His Church. This is why unity and indissolubility are a characteristic of true marriage and suffer no exception, even when a couple is not blessed with children.

What St. Paul says about marriage in his Letter to the Ephesians can only confirm the traditional teaching of the Church, according to which Matrimony is one of the Sacraments instituted by Christ. Being a Sacrament, it is for the spouses a source of grace: the grace they need to fulfil their obligations towards each other and towards their children in spite of the weakness of human nature.

The New Testament gives us an example of Christians who sanctified their marriage. Aquila and Priscilla, converts from Judaism, actively cooperated with St. Paul in spreading the Faith, first in Corinth then in Ephesus. Without doing anything strange, they made of their work and their social life an opportunity of bringing others closer to Christ (cf. Acts 18:1-3;18-19;24-28).

St. Peter has left us a brief, but beautiful description of the peace and joy that reign in a Christian family when the wife is seeking to create a bright and cheerful home, respecting the authority of the head of the family; the husband, on his part, loves and respects his wife and seeks her happiness, so that in fact he never takes serious decisions concerning the family without considering his wife's opinion. *You, too, who are wives must be submissive to your husbands. Some of these still refuse credence to the word; it is for their wives to win them over, not by word but by example; by the modesty and reverence they observe in your demeanour. Your beauty must lie, not in braided hair, not in gold trinkets, not in the dress you wear, but in the hidden features of your hearts, in a possession you can never lose, that of a calm and tranquil spirit; to God's eyes, beyond price. It was thus that the holy women of old time adorned themselves, those women who had such trust in God, and paid their husbands such respect.*

Think how obedient Sara was to Abraham, how she called him her Lord; if you would prove yourselves her children, live honestly, and let no anxious thoughts disturb you. You, too, who are husbands must use marriage considerately, paying homage to woman's sex as weaker than your own. The grace of eternal life belongs to both, and your prayers must not suffer interruption (1 Peter 3:1-7).

In such an atmosphere of authentic love and respect, the children can be brought up as good Christians; the parents will correct them rather than punish them, teaching them what is right and what is wrong. *You who are children must show obedience in the Lord to your parents; it is your duty; Honour thy father and thy mother – that is the first commandment which has a promise attached to it, So that it shall go well with thee, and thou shalt live long to enjoy the land. You who are fathers, do not rouse your children to resentment; the training, the discipline in which you bring them up must come from the Lord* (Eph. 6:1-4).

Education in the Faith should start in childhood. Then parents are laying a solid foundation upon which their children can build up a strong Christian life. This is why St. Paul was able to tell Timothy, whose mother and grandmother were Christians: *Thou canst remember the holy learning thou hast been taught from childhood upwards. This will train thee up for salvation, through the faith which rests in Christ Jesus* (2 Tim. 3:15).

8

Mary, Mother of the Church

So, in his spite against the woman, the dragon went elsewhere to make war on the rest her children, the men who keep God's commandments, and hold fast to the truth concerning Jesus (Apoc. 12:17).

To know the truth about the Mother of the Saviour, we need more than ever the Tradition of the Church. Part of that Tradition was written in the books of the New Testament. A great deal remained unwritten, but was transmitted orally and was eventually defined by the Teaching Authority of the Church as part of the deposit of the Faith.

Holy Scripture says little about Our Lady. Yet what it does say is loaded with meaning. Revealed truth need not be explicitly stated. God gave men a mind, which is like a spark of the divine Intelligence, so that they should make use of it to examine certain revealed facts, see their relation to one another, and draw the logical consequences. In other words, God expects us 'to put two and two together'.

Holy Scripture implies, rather than states, the greatness of Mary. Quite a few texts give some indications of her attributes, but they are not perfectly clear, and they need Tradition to clarify their full significance. The Church is the lawful interpreter of the Bible, and its Tradition gives light to otherwise obscure texts. Tradition never contradicts the written word. On the contrary, it uncovers the depth and beauty of its meaning. Tradition and Holy Scripture both contain God's revelation and complement each other.

Mother of God

And behold, thou shalt conceive in thy womb, and shalt bear a son, and shalt call him Jesus. He shall be great, and men will know him for the Son of the Most High; the Lord God will give him the throne of his father David, and he shall reign over the house of Jacob eternally; his kingdom shall never have an end (Luke 1:31-34).

Jesus is the Second Person of the Holy Trinity, therefore He is God. He truly became a man, taking His human nature from a woman. *Then God sent out his Son on a mission to us. He took birth from a woman, took birth as a subject of the law* (Gal. 4:4). St. John is even more explicit on the fact that Jesus is True God: *At the beginning of time the Word already was; and God had the Word abiding with him, and the Word was God*

(John 1:1); this divine Word became man: *And the Word was made flesh, and came to dwell among us; and we had sight of his glory, glory such as belongs to the Father's only-begotten Son, full of grace and truth* (John 1:14).

The words of the Angel announce the imminent fulfilment of Isaias' prophecy: *For our sakes a child is born, to our race a son is given, whose shoulder will bear the sceptre of princely power. What name shall be given him? Peerless among counsellors, the mighty God, Father of the world to come, the Prince of Peace. Ever wider shall his dominion spread, endlessly at peace; he will sit on David's kingly throne, to give it lasting foundations of justice and right, so tenderly he loves us, the Lord of hosts* (Is. 9:6-7). His kingdom will have no end, therefore He must be God, for nothing earthly can last for ever.

In Jesus then we find two natures: the divine and the human natures. There is, however, only one person, that of the Son. 'Nature' answers the question *what*: what is Jesus Christ? He is both God and Man (two natures). 'Person' answers the question *who*: who is Jesus Christ? The Second Person of the Holy Trinity. The pronoun *I* necessarily refers to a person, and Jesus said: *My Father and I are one* (John 10:30). He could not have said this if there had been within Him a distinction of persons between Christ the Man and Christ Son of God.

Mary is the Mother of Jesus. Like all human mothers, she is the mother of a person, not only of a nature. It would be unthinkable for any woman to say: 'I am not the mother of little Johnnie, I only gave birth to his human nature'. Why then make such affirmation in the case of Mary? She gave birth to a person, who is a divine Person. Jesus is God, and so, while it is partly correct to say that Mary gave birth to a human child (for Jesus is true Man), we must acknowledge her as Mother of God made man (for Jesus is true God). As the Incarnation of the Son of God did not diminish in any way His divinity, Mary is rightly called Mother of God.

A basic knowledge of philosophy is enough to understand this truth revealed by God and taught by the Church: that God, eternal being and creator of heaven and earth, could decide to be born from a woman, who would therefore be mother of her Creator. God did not receive his divine nature, but only his human nature, from her. There is, however, only one Christ, who is both God and Man. The reasoning made by the Church is very simple and follows the strictest rules of logic: Mary is the mother of Christ, Christ is God, therefore Mary is Mother of God.

All other perfections attributed to Mary are consequences of her divine Motherhood. They do not need to be expressly mentioned in Holy Scripture. They were part of the Christian belief from the beginning, although they were stated and explained in detail progressively, as heresies appeared and showed the need for a definition of Faith. The Bible, however, gives us some indications that confirm the teachings of the Church with regard to Our Lady.

Conceived without sin

> *Hail, thou who art full of grace; the Lord is with thee; blessed art thou among women* (Luke 1:28).

The first revelation concerning Mary is to be found at the beginning of the Book of Genesis. After Adam and Eve had sinned and lost God's friendship, God promised a Saviour who would be born of a woman. Addressing the devil, God said: *And I will establish a feud between thee and the woman, between thy offspring and hers; she* is to crush thy head, while thou dost lie in ambush at her heels* (Gen. 3:15).

It is possible that the prophecy refers in a direct way to Eve, whose posterity would eventually include the Saviour who would overcome the devil. But this does not prevent it from referring to Mary as well, this particular descendent of Eve who was to give birth to Christ.

The Mother of God could not possibly be associated with the devil for a single moment. Any sin,

---

* The original Hebrew text says *he* instead of *she*. Even if the *she* is the result of a copying error, it does not really alter the sense of the passage. Christ is the seed of the woman, as well as the seed, the offspring, of Abraham (cf. Gal. 3:16). If we are united to Him, we are also Abraham's offspring: *And if you belong to Christ, then you are indeed Abraham's children; the promised inheritance is yours* (Gal. 3:29). There is such union of hearts between Mary and Jesus that the Son's victory is shared by the Mother.

even if it is not a personal one, implies a certain
subjection to Satan. It is repugnant to the mind to think
that Jesus could have received His humanity from a
mother who had, even for only an instant, been
subjected to God's bitterest enemy. The teaching of the
Church on the Immaculate Conception of Mary, i.e. the
fact that she was conceived without original sin, full of
grace from the very moment of her conception, is fully
in accord with this first prophecy pronounced by God
Himself. Mary is the Woman in whom Satan finds his
most implacable enemy and who will indeed crush his
head through the Redemption achieved by her Son.

The realisation of this prophecy is confirmed by
the words of the Angel Gabriel to Mary: *Hail, thou who
art full of grace; the Lord is with thee; blessed art thou
among women* (Luke 1:28). Some prefer to translate
'highly favoured' instead of 'full of grace'. As it has
already been explained in Chapter six, the words
'grace' and 'favour' are identical in Greek. They have
in fact the same meaning. The word 'highly' is not
really appropriate as the Greek word
'χεΧαριτωμενη' conveys an idea of plenitude; the
expression *full of grace* could possibly be rendered as
filled with favour or *possessing the fullness of God's
favour*, which is eventually the same as the more
traditional expression *full of grace*.

The concept of fullness of grace, plenitude of
God's favour, leaves no room at all for sin. Original sin,
even when it has been eliminated by Baptism, leaves its
scar on the soul, something we could compare with a
crack in a water pot, causing some of the water to leak
and be wasted. Personal sins make the situation worse,
causing a serious wastage, and often a complete loss, of

God's grace, and making the soul displeasing to God. No, there could be no trace of sin in the Woman filled with grace, whose offspring would win a complete victory over the devil.

Moreover, the rest of the Angel's greeting to Mary is worth underlining. He tells her: *The Lord is with thee*. This is very surprising when one takes into account that the normal Jewish practice was to make a wish, not a statement. *The Lord be with thee*, an angel had said to Gedeon (Judges 6:12)). *The Lord be with thee*, Saul had said to David (1 Kings 17:37). The Apostles used variations of this expression, always in the form of a wish: *Grace and peace be yours from God, our Father, and from the Lord Jesus Christ* (1 Cor. 1:3; 2 Cor. 1:2; Gal. 1:3; Eph. 1:3 etc.), *Grace and peace be yours abundantly* (1 Peter 1:2; 2 Peter 1:1), *Mercy and peace and love be yours, in full measure* (Jude 1:2).

If the Angel, God's messenger, told Mary *The Lord is with thee*, it was to indicate a very special degree of holiness, the absence of any sin that could have endangered the presence of God in her soul. There was no need to wish her union with God: such union was already a deep, permanent, unshakable reality.

Moreover Elizabeth, filled with the Holy Spirit, makes a parallel between the blessing of God resting upon Mary, and the blessing of God resting upon Christ in His humanity, thus suggesting that Mary, like Christ, was free from sin from the beginning of her existence: *Blessed art thou among women, and blessed is the fruit of thy womb* (Luke 1:41).

Virgin for ever

> *All this was so ordained to fulfil the word*
> *which the Lord spoke by his prophet:*
> *Behold, the virgin shall be with child, and*
> *shall bear a son, and they shall call him*
> *Emmanuel* (*which means, God with us*)
> (Matt. 1:22-23).

According to Isaias, God gave Achaz, king of
Israel, a sign of His favour: *Maid shall be with child,*
and shall bear a son, that shall be called Emmanuel (Is.
7:14). The Hebrew word 'almah' means a young
unmarried girl; it does not literally mean *virgin* but it is
equivalent to it considering the relatively strict moral
code of the Jews. This prophecy was fulfilled in Mary.
The name Emmanuel was never given to Jesus, but if
we remember that among the Jews, a name was
supposed to indicate an essential truth about a person,
it is easy to see that Jesus, the Second Person of the
Holy Trinity made man, has greater claim than anyone
else to the name of Emmanuel, for He truly is *God*
with us.

Mary was a virgin when she conceived Christ and
gave Him birth. She asked the Angel: *How can that be,*
since I have no knowledge of man (Luke 1:34). Since
she was betrothed to Joseph, this question would make
little sense if she had not resolved to preserve her
virginity. Mary's question, moreover, was not an
expression of doubt. There is a world of difference
between the reaction of Zachary and that of Mary to
the message received from God. Zachary did not hide
his scepticism: *and Zachary said to the angel, By what*

sign am I to be assured of this? I am an old man now, and my wife is far advanced in age (Luke 1:18). Mary simply asked how this would take place, so that she could understand what was expected of her, and so fulfil the will of God better.

When giving the genealogy of Jesus, St. Matthew changes style abruptly when he reaches Joseph's relationship with the Redeemer: ... *and Jacob was the father of Joseph, the husband of Mary; it was of her that Jesus was born, who is called Christ* (Matt. 1:16). Several women apart from Mary are mentioned in this genealogy, but in an incidental way. We read that Juda was the father of Phares and Zara, by Thamar; Salmon of Booz, by Rahab; Booz of Obed, by Ruth; David of Solomon, by the wife of Urias. In those cases, the emphasis is placed on the fatherhood of the man. In the case of the Redeemer, Joseph is not called father of Jesus, but husband of Mary, and the emphasis is placed on the motherhood of Mary. This is at least a strong indication of the virginal birth of Christ, confirmed by the genealogy given to us by St. Luke and which states that Jesus *was, by repute, son of Joseph* (Luke 3:23).

The birth of Jesus did not affect the virginity of His Mother. If we know how to read between the lines, we can understand that Mary did not give birth in suffering. *With pangs thou shalt give birth to children* (Gen. 3:16); the sufferings of childbirth are a direct consequence of original sin, and Mary was as free from them as she was free from sin. The Gospel account of Jesus' birth gives an impression of great peace and serenity; we cannot imagine an ordinary birth when we read that *she brought forth a son, her first-born, whom she wrapped in his swaddling clothes, and laid in a*

manger, because there was no room for them in the inn
(Luke 2:7). Mary needed no assistance to attend to the
immediate needs of the new-born Child.

Several objections have been put forward to deny
the perpetual virginity of Mary in which Christians have
firmly believed from the very beginning of the life of
the Church. A basic knowledge of Jewish customs and
turns of speech is enough to refute them.

Both St. Luke and St. Matthew mention that Jesus
was Mary's first-born son. One may be tempted to
jump to the conclusion that if He was the first, then
there must have been others after him. This, however,
would only show ignorance of Jewish traditions.
According to the Law of Moses, every first-born child
or animal was to be dedicated to God, and this custom
was to last as long as the Covenant between God and
Israel: *and when the Lord has made good his promise to*
thee and to thy fathers, by bringing thee into the
Chanaanite land and giving it to thee for thy own, thou
shalt dedicate to the Lord the first-born of every womb,
the first-fruits of all thy cattle; every such thing, if it be of
the male sex, is forfeit to him. When an ass has its first
foal, thou shalt offer a sheep in payment of its ransom; if
not, it must be killed. And every first-born man child of
thy own race shall have a price paid for his ransom.
When, in after times, thy sons ask thee what is the
meaning of this, thou shalt tell them how the Lord's
constraining power rescued you from your prison-house
in Egypt, how Pharao's heart was hardened, and he
would not let you go free, until the Lord slew every first-
born male thing, man or beast, in the Land of Egypt.
That (thou shalt say) is why I immolate to the Lord
every first-born thing, the first-fruits of every womb,

except among my own children; and for these I must pay ransom; this custom is to endure like a mark branded on the hand, to be kept in view like a badge worn on the forehead, to remind you, too, how the Lord's constraining power rescued us from Egypt (Ex. 13:11-16). So the term *first-born son* indicates that there was no other child before, but it makes absolutely no reference to the future. Because Mary had had no child before Jesus, Jesus had all the rights and duties attached to a first-born son, and His parents had to pay a ransom for Him: *and so they must offer in sacrifice for him, as God's law commanded, a pair of turtle-doves, or two young pigeons* (Luke 2:24).

On several occasions, we also hear about the brothers and sisters of Jesus. *How did he come by this wisdom, and these strange powers? Is not this the carpenter's son, whose mother is called Mary, and his brethren James and Joseph and Simon and Judas? And do not his sisters, all of them, live near us? How is it that all this has come to him?* (Matt. 13:54-56). This cannot be a problem for anyone who is familiar with the Jewish customs or with certain social systems as, for example, the African society. In the language of the Jews as in African languages, there are no special terms for the various degrees of family relationships: all members of a family such as cousins and nephews are included under the name *brother* or *sister*. The Bible bears testimony of this when calling Lot and Abraham *brethren* (Gen. 13:8) after having explained that Lot was a nephew of Abraham, the son of his brother Aran: *Thare's sons were called Abraham, Nachor and Aran, and Aran had a son called Lot* (Gen. 13:8). The *brothers and sisters* of Jesus were simply relations.

Finally, another objection to the perpetual virginity of Mary arises from a misunderstanding of the Jewish meaning of the word *'till'* or *'until'*. The literal translation of Matt. 1:25 is: (*Joseph*) *knew her not till she bore a son*. In English, this sentence immediately suggests that, once she had borne her son, Joseph did know her. However, this is not the case in Hebrew, which is the language in which St. Matthew originally wrote his Gospel. In Hebrew, the word *until* or *till* only makes reference to the time that has passed before the occurrence of an event; it does not imply that a change took place after that event. The Bible gives evidence of this: *The Lord said to my Lord: Sit thou at my right hand until I make thy enemies thy footstool* (Ps. 109:1); yet we know that Christ sits at the right hand of God for ever. *And they went up to mount Sion with joy and gladness, and offered holocausts, because not one of them was slain, till they had returned in peace* (1 Mac. 5:54); it is obvious that they were not slain after they had returned in peace. A more modern translation of the Bible such as the Ronald Knox version transmits the real meaning of the text instead of the literal translation indicated above: *Sit here at my right hand while I make thy enemies a footstool under thy feet* and *they offered burnt-sacrifice in thanks for their safe home-coming, with never a life lost*. Keeping this in mind, Matt. 1:25 is best translated as: (*Joseph*) *had not known her when she bore a son, her first-born*. It is not a deformation of the passage, but a translation of its true sense. The literal translation is not incorrect, but it is ambiguous at times and, even though it is understood by scholars, it can be confusing for less learned men.

There are other examples in the New Testament. St. Paul's recommendation to Timothy, *Till I come, attend unto reading, to exhortation and to doctrine* (1 Tim. 4:13), cannot possibly be restricted to the periods of absence of the Apostle. St. Paul was only asking him not to forget, in his absence, these essential occupations of the priestly ministry. In modern English he would say *while I am absent* rather than *till I come*.

We can also bring forward arguments of common sense to justify the Church's belief in the perpetual virginity of Christ's Mother. The Woman announced by God through the Prophets, the Woman who was chosen from all eternity to conceive the Son of God and give Him birth in His human nature, the Woman who had become the Spouse of the Holy Spirit, was not going to conceive other children from a human spouse. Such an idea is repugnant to the mind. The Book of Ezechiel gives us, if not a proof, at least a confirmation of how reasonable it was for Mary to remain a virgin for ever. *Then he brought me back to the eastern gate of the outer precincts, that was fast shut. Shut this gate must ever be, the Lord told me, nor open its doors to give man entrance again, since the Lord, the God of Israel, entered by it* (Ez. 44:1-2). Because the power of God had once passed through this particular city gate, no man was permitted to make use of it ever after, for it was considered sacred and had to be reserved to God alone. The same reasoning applies with even greater force to the Virgin Mary. *The Holy Spirit will come upon thee, and the power of the Most High will overshadow thee. Thus this holy offspring of thine shall be known for the Son of God* (Luke 1:35). The womb in which the body of the Son of God was formed through a very special intervention of the Holy Spirit was sanctified by the divine Presence and consecrated to God; it belonged to God alone.

St. Joseph, who was *a just man*, i.e. a pious and holy Jew, understood very well that his great privilege was to look after the Saviour's Holy Mother and to be a father to Jesus, and that this privilege required renouncing having children of his own.

The Jews considered it a moral and a religious duty to beget children. To understand how St. Joseph could possibly consent to preserve Mary's virginity, we must take several factors into account: his eminent holiness, the special graces God certainly gave him to enable him fulfil his mission, his pure love for Mary, which led him to respect her desire to consecrate herself to God, and finally his deep-rooted veneration for the sacredness of God's presence. Moreover, the reason why marriage and children were so important to the Jews was the hope of being counted among the ancestors of the Messiah. Once Jesus, the promised Redeemer, had come to the home of Mary and Joseph, hope had become a reality; the natural desire of having children lost all strength compared with the undeniable fact of God's very special presence in Mary. For Joseph, to beget children through her would have been an unjustifiable desecration.

Co-redemptrix with Christ

> *As for thy own soul, it shall have a sword to pierce it* (Luke 2:35).

Mary was closely associated to the redemptive work of her Son. God sent the Archangel Gabriel to let her know His plan for Her and obtain her consent. Simeon, led by the Holy Spirit, revealed to her that her Son would be rejected by many and that she would share in His suffering. *Behold, this child is destined to bring about the fall of many and the rise of many in Israel; to be a sign which men will refuse to acknowledge; and so the thoughts of many hearts shall be made manifest; as for thy own soul, it shall have a sword to pierce it* (Luke 2:34-35). She must have been well aware of the growing hostility of the Jews from Judaea towards Jesus, and it must have made her suffer very much She was present in Jerusalem when her Son was arrested, condemned and executed. She must have heard the shouts of the crowd, *Crucify him, crucify him* (John 19:6), and seen her Son after the scourging, wearing a crown of thorns. The Bible tells us that she was present at the Crucifixion: *his mother, and his mother's sister, Mary the wife of Cleophas, and Mary Magdalen, had taken their stand beside the Cross of Jesus* (John 19:25).

It is easy to imagine Mary's sorrow when contemplating her Son on the Cross. St. Paul tells us something that suggests that her sorrow in union with Christ's suffering implied a close association of the Mother in the redemptive work of the Son. He compares Christ with Adam: Christ is the second Adam who undid with his obedience what the first one had done with his disobedience. *It was through one man that guilt came into the world; and, since death came owing to guilt, death was handed on to all mankind by one man ... In this, Adam was the type of him who was to come. Only, the grace which came to us was out of all proportion to the fault. If this one man's fault brought death on a whole multitude, all the more lavish was God's grace, shown to a whole multitude, that free gift he made us in the grace brought by one man, Jesus Christ* (Rom. 5:12:14-15).

We read in the Book of Genesis that Eve was first led by pride to disobedience, although the original sin was not fully consummated until Adam himself followed her example. When we look upon Christ as the second Adam, it is logical that we should seek a second Eve called to share through her humility and obedience, in the redeeming Passion of the Saviour. We can easily find her in the Woman who gave her consent to the Incarnation of the Son of God and who accompanied Him during the sorrowful hours of His Passion and Death, in total submission to the Will of God.

Model of virtues

> *Blessed are those who hear the word of God and keep it* (Luke 11:28).

St. Luke tells us that, as Jesus was preaching to the crowds *when he spoke thus, a woman in the multitude said to him aloud: Blessed is the womb that bore thee, the breast which thou hast sucked. And he answered, Shall we not say, Blessed are those who hear the word of God, and keep it?* (Luke 11:27-28).

These words are sometimes taken as a denial, on the part of Christ, of any special dignity attached to His

Mother. But this is not so. The woman in the crowd, with solid peasant common sense, understood that the dignity of the Son meant great honour for the Mother. Jesus wanted to raise her praise of Mary to a higher, supernatural level. He pointed out that, more than the blood relation in itself, it was her eminent degree of holiness that made Mary stand out among all others. Who heard the word of God more attentively and keep it more faithfully than Mary? The first time we meet her in the pages of the Gospel, she listens carefully to the message of the Angel, asks a question to understand exactly what is expected from her, and says: *Behold the handmaid of the Lord; let it be done unto me according to thy word* (Luke 1:38).

Having heard from the Angel that her cousin Elizabeth is expecting a child in her old age, she immediately takes the hint and goes to stay with her for three months so that she can be of service to her in the last stage of her pregnancy. Inspired by the Holy Spirit, Elizabeth praises Mary for her Faith: *Blessed art thou for thy believing* (Luke 1:45), and Mary cannot refrain from singing for joy, acknowledging with deep humility her own smallness and God's greatness: *My soul magnifies the Lord; my spirit has found joy in God, who is my Saviour, because he has looked graciously upon the lowliness of his handmaid. Behold, from this day forward all generations will count me blessed, because he who is mighty, he whose name is holy, has wrought for me his wonders* (Luke 1:46-49).

Mary tries to discover the will of God manifested in the events of her life. On two occasions the Gospel makes reference to her interior life, her spirit of meditation and contemplation. After the shepherds had explained what they had been told about the Child, *Mary treasured up all these sayings, and reflected on them in her heart* (Luke 2:19). During the long years Jesus spent in Nazareth with Mary and Joseph (He was over 30 years old when He started His public life), *he lived there in subjection to them, while his mother kept in her heart the memory of all this* (Luke 2:51).

She never lost hope. Already at the wedding feast of Cana, she had manifested her unshakable trust in her divine Son's power and mercy when, after His apparent rebuke, she had told the servants: *Do whatever he tells you* (John 2:5). After Jesus' Crucifixion and burial, she does not return to the tomb with the Holy Women; she does not join them to go and embalm the body of her Son. How can this be explained? She had understood Jesus' prediction of the Resurrection and she patiently waited for Him to rise from the dead, as He had said.

She surely did not take offence when Jesus declared: *who is a mother, who are brethren to me? Then he stretched out his hand towards his disciples, and said, Here are my mother and my brethren! If anyone does the will of my Father who is in heaven, he is my brother, and sister, and mother* (Matt. 12:48-50). She who considered herself as the handmaid of the Lord, deserved more than any one else the title of mother, for no-one ever fulfilled the will of God the Father as faithfully and lovingly as she did. These words of Christ may have prepared her for the role of Mother of all men she would have to assume later on, for Jesus was announcing that He would have many brothers and sisters in a spiritual sense.

The Virgin of Nazareth was always ready to do the

will of God and, as we have already seen, to love God means to observe His commandments.

Faith, Hope, Charity, Humility, Obedience ... In fact, all virtues shine in Mary as we see her through the pages of the Gospel. Temperance: she practised chastity and detachment from the goods of this world in Bethlehem, Egypt, Nazareth, Capharnaum and Jerusalem, following in the footsteps of Christ. Fortitude: she stood at the foot of the Cross when all the Apostles except John had run away. Prudence: she identified herself with the will of God and taught others to do the same: *Do whatever he tells you* (John 2:5). Justice: she rendered God the glory due to Him and was among those who hunger and thirst for justice, i.e. for holiness. *My soul magnifies the Lord; my spirit has found joy in God, who is my Saviour, because he has looked graciously upon the lowliness of his handmaid. Behold, from this day forward all generations will count me blessed; because he who is mighty, he whose name is holy, has wrought for me his wonders* ... (Luke 1:46-49 ss.).

Queen of heaven

> *And now, in heaven, a great portent appeared; a woman that wore the sun for her mantle, with the moon under her feet, and a crown of twelve stars about her head. She had a child in her womb, and was crying out as she travailed, in great pain of her delivery. Then a second*

portent appeared in heaven; a great
dragon was there, fiery-red, with seven
heads and ten horns, and on each of the
seven heads a royal diadem; his tail
dragged down a third part of the stars in
heaven, and flung them to earth.

And he stood fronting the woman who
was in childbirth, ready to swallow up the
child as soon as she bore it. She bore a
son, the son who is to herd the nations
like sheep with a crook of iron; and this
child of hers was caught up to God, right
up to his throne, while the mother fled
into the wilderness, where God had
prepared a place of refuge for her; and
there, for twelve hundred and sixty days,
she is to be kept safe (Apoc. 12:1-6).

Who is this Woman the Apostle John saw,
crowned with glory, in heaven? The Child, who is to
herd the nations like sheep with a crook of iron and
was caught up to God's throne, is evidently Christ. The
dragon is, in John's own words, the *serpent of the primal*
age ..., *he whom we call the devil, or Satan, the whole*
world's seducer (Apoc. 12:9). The Woman whom the
devil cannot conquer reminds us of the first messianic
prophecy contained in the Book of Genesis: *and I will*
establish a feud between thee and the woman, between
thy offspring and hers; she is to crush thy head, while
thou dost lie in ambush at her heels (Gen. 3:15).
Christian Tradition has always seen in this Woman a
symbol of the Church which must go through great
suffering in order to bring Christ to the souls of men.

But Mary herself is a figure of the Church: Virgin Mother, who brings us Christ and helps souls to find Christ.

St. John could not fail to see Mary in this Woman, Mother of the Messiah, in her struggle with the devil: Mary, the second Eve, defeating the devil with the help of God. *So the dragon, finding himself cast down to earth, went in pursuit of the woman, the boy's mother; but the woman was given two wings, such as the great eagle has, to speed her flight into the wilderness, to her place of refuge, where for a year, and two years, and half a year, she will be kept hidden from the serpent's view. Thereupon the serpent sent a flood of water out of his mouth in pursuit of the woman, to carry her away on its tide; but earth came to the woman's rescue. The earth gaped wide, and swallowed up this flood which the dragon had sent out of his mouth* (Apoc. 12:13-16).

Although there is no direct reference to the Assumption of Mary into Heaven and her crowning as Queen of all Creation, the Catholic Tradition on these, derived from the doctrine of the Immaculate Conception and the divine Motherhood of Mary, is somehow confirmed by this picture the Bible offers us of Mary, image of the Church, clothed with the sun and crowned with twelve stars, with the moon under her feet.

Mother of the Church

And meanwhile his mother, and his mother's sister, Mary the wife of

> *Cleophas, and Mary Magdalen, had taken their stand beside the cross of Jesus. And Jesus, seeing his mother there, and the disciple, too, whom he loved, standing by, said to his mother, Woman, this is thy son.*
>
> *Then he said to the disciple, This is thy mother. And from that hour the disciple took her into his own keeping* (John 19:25-27).

As Jesus was dying on the Cross, He had a last manifestation of love for His mother. Considering the position of the woman in Jewish society, she needed protection: life could be very hard for a widow in the land of Israel, especially if she had no grown up son. Seeing her with John, the youngest Apostle, He entrusted them to each other's care.

The words of Jesus: *This is thy son, this is thy mother* do not establish a relation only between Mary and John. They also concern us. Jesus was fully aware of His Mission until the very last moment and had no other thought but that of fulfilling the task appointed to Him by His Father. Every word He pronounced on the Cross was part of His redeeming mission. When He told Mary to be a Mother to John, He made her Mother of all Christians, indeed of all men.

Jesus' words must have caused a deep impression on John. John, son of Zebedee, was not an orphan. His own mother was present on Golgotha, accompanying the suffering Lord. She was probably only a few paces away from him. St. Matthew tells us that *many women stood watching from far off; they had followed Jesus from Galilee, to minister to him; among them were Mary Magdalen, and Mary the mother of James and Joseph, and the mother of the sons of Zebedee* (Matt. 27:55-56). Mark tells us that her name was Salome (cf. Mark 15:40). Did she hear Jesus' words? We do not know. But John certainly understood the spiritual sense of this mother-son relationship that was to exist between Mary and himself. Mary understood it even better, and she kept her Son's disciples together, strengthening their Faith and Hope. The Acts of the Apostles show us the disciples gathered around Mary, praying, hoping, waiting for the coming of the Holy Spirit. *Coming in, they went up into the upper room where they dwelt, Peter and John, James and Andrew, Philip and Thomas, Bartholomew and Matthew, James the son of Alphaeus and Simon the Zealot, and Judas the brother of James. All these, with one mind, gave themselves up to prayer, together with Mary the mother of Jesus, and the rest of the women and his brethren* (Acts 1:13-14).

The teachings of St. Paul on the Church, Mystical Body of Christ, throw light on this new Motherhood of Mary. *He has put everything under his dominion, and made him the head to which the whole Church is joined, so that the Church is his body, the completion of him who everywhere and in all things is complete* (Eph. 1:22-23). We, Christians, are one with Christ. Christ had expressed this truth when telling Saul on the way to Damascus: *I am Jesus, whom Saul persecutes* (Acts 9:5). We form one body with Christ as our head. *We are to follow the truth in a spirit of charity, and so grow up, in everything, into a due proportion with Christ, who is our head. On him all the body depends; it is organised and unified by each contact with the source which supplies it; and thus, each limb receiving the active power it needs, it achieves its natural growth, building itself up through charity* (Eph. 4:15-16).

Mary is the Mother of Jesus. Jesus lives not only in Himself, but in His Church, which is like a continuation of His own Body. He is the Head, the Church is His Mystical Body. Mary is Mother of the whole Christ: Mother of Jesus according to the flesh, she became the spiritual Mother of His Mystical Body, the Church. This is the full meaning of Jesus' words on the Cross: *Woman, this is thy son, this is thy mother.*

Indeed Mary gave birth to us, spiritually, at the foot of the Cross, with great suffering. There she became Mother of the Church.

Years later, John saw a vision in the sky, *a woman that wore the sun for her mantle, with the moon under her feet, and a crown of twelve stars about her head. She had a child in her womb, and was crying out as she travailed, in great pain of her delivery* (Apoc. 12:1-2). We have already seen that this Woman represents both the Church and Mary. Mary, who gave birth to Jesus virginally and without suffering, became the Mother of men through an agony of suffering, following in the footsteps of Her divine Son. The vision described in the Apocalypse presents her to us as Mother of the Messiah and also of a vast multitude: *so, in his spite against the woman, the dragon went elsewhere to make war on the rest of her children, the men who keep God's commandments and hold fast to the truth concerning Jesus* (Apoc. 12:17). We are included among *the rest of her children* if we keep God's commandments and believe faithfully in the truths of Faith presented to us by the Church, Bride of Christ and therefore One with

Him. In this sense, it is true that Mary has many children beside Jesus, for Christ became, in the words of Scripture, *the eldest-born among many brethren* (Rom. 8:29). Christ is first of all Son of God, but He is also truly son of Mary. When He died on the Cross, He made us children of God, and He precisely chose that moment to give us His Mother to be ours.

And from that hour the disciple took her into his own keeping (John 19:27). We, too, must show ourselves children of God and children of Mary. We, too, must take her into our own home. To reject her, to refuse to take her as our Mother, means to go directly against the express will of the dying Redeemer.

Devotion to Mary

> *And Elizabeth herself was filled with the Holy Ghost; so that she cried out with a loud voice, Blessed art thou among women, and blessed is the fruit of thy womb. How have I deserved to be thus visited by the mother of my Lord?* (Luke 1:41-43).

Devotion to the Virgin Mary, Mother of God, is as old as the events narrated in the Gospels. St. Matthew certainly did not consider her as an ordinary person when he told us that *she was found to be with child by the power of the Holy Ghost* (Matt. 1:18) and when he let us know that she was the virgin Isaias foretold, who would be the Mother of a child called *God-with-us*. St.

Luke also speaks of her with great respect; he dedicates two full chapters to the events immediately preceding the Incarnation of Christ and to the childhood of Jesus, showing us Mary as a woman full of grace, filled with the Holy Spirit, attentive to the word of God and docile to His inspirations.

The first person to address words of praise to Mary was a special messenger from God, the Archangel Gabriel. It is interesting to compare the attitude of Gabriel towards Mary with that of angels sent by God to other persons such as Abraham (cf. Gen. 18:1-22), Gedeon (cf. Judges 6:11-21), Samson's parents (cf. Judges 13:2-21) or Zachary (cf. Luke 1:11-20). Gabriel speaks with great respect to Mary, and we must not forget that the words he pronounces are not his own, but God's message: *Hail, thou who art full of grace; the Lord is with thee; blessed art thou among women* (Luke 1:28). If God judged it appropriate to exalt Mary above all women, who are we to deny her this honour?

Next we hear Elizabeth's greeting to her cousin. Let us keep in mind that in Jewish as well as in African society, great importance is attached to age and special respect is due to older persons. Mary was very young; Elizabeth was already old. According to the rules of proper behaviour, Mary greeted her cousin first. However, the Gospel tells us that Elizabeth, filled with the Holy Spirit, addressed her young relative with a respect and even veneration that could have no human explanation. *No sooner had Elizabeth heard Mary's greeting, than the child leaped in her womb; and Elizabeth herself was filled with the Holy Ghost; so that she cried out with a loud voice, Blessed art thou among women, and blessed is the fruit of thy womb. How have I deserved to be thus visited by the mother of my Lord?* (Luke 1:41-43). The Holy Spirit made Elizabeth understand the greatness of Mary, her sublime dignity as the mother of the Lord, i.e. of God. And we too, if we are led by the Holy Spirit, can only marvel at having Jesus' Mother as ours and we too should exclaim: *How have I deserved to be thus visited by the mother of my Lord!* Devotion to Mary is one facet of devotion to Christ.

Any time we repeat the first part of the Hail Mary, we address the Holy Virgin with the same words God addressed to her on the day of the Anunciation, the same words the Holy Spirit inspired Elizabeth on the day of the Visitation. In the second part of the Hail Mary, we ask her to pray for us sinners, now and at the hour of our death.

How deeply evangelical such a prayer is: with words God Himself taught us, and asking for prayers from someone closer to God than we are! How often Jesus performed miracles for someone at the petition of a third person! He cured the servant of the centurion (cf. Matt. 8:5-13), the daughter of the Syrophenician woman (cf. Matt. 15:21-28) and the palsied man brought by friends to the feet of Jesus (cf. Luke 5:18-26); He raised Jairus' daughter from the dead (cf. Matt. 9:18-26) as well as Lazarus (cf. John 11:1-44), each time at the request of a relative or a friend. Why should we not ask Mary, the Mother of Jesus, to pray for us, to ask graces, favours, for us from God who cannot fail to look with favour upon the Woman who always heard the word of God and kept it?

Jesus must have loved His mother very much, for

He fulfilled the Commandments better than anyone else and certainly did not exclude the Fourth Commandment: *Honour thy father and thy mother.* He was and still is perfect God and perfect Man. Who could call perfect a man who has neither love nor respect for his mother? Like all good sons, Jesus is pleased if we praise His Mother, displeased if we neglect or *snub* her.

St. John tells us an anecdote that shows the power of Mary's intercession. *There was a wedding feast at Cana, in Galilee; and Jesus' mother was there. Jesus himself, and his disciples, had also been invited to the wedding. Here the supply of wine failed; whereupon Jesus' mother said to him, They have no wine left. Jesus answered her, Nay, woman, why dost thou trouble me with that? My time has not come yet. And his mother said to the servants, Do whatever he tells you. There were six water-pots standing there, as the Jewish custom of ceremonial washing demanded; they were of stone, and held two or three firkins apiece. And when Jesus said, Fill the water-pots with water, they filled these up to the brim. Then he said to them, Now draw, and give a draught to the master of the feast. So they gave it to him; and the master of the feast tasted this water, which had now been turned into wine. He did not know whence it came; only the servants who had drawn the water knew that* (John 2:1-9). Mary did not need to be told about the problem; she noticed it before anyone else, because she cared for the happiness of others. She did not start criticising the bride's family for their lack of foresight; she simply told Jesus about the problem, not formulating any petition, knowing that Jesus would understand very well her silent plea. She was not put off by her Son's apparent rebuff. She knew He would not deny her anything. And so she told the servants they should do anything He asked them to do. And indeed Jesus took action and performed a miracle.

The power of Mary's intercession! We can be sure she intercedes for us too. But if we want to obtain miracles, we have to follow her advice. When addressing the servants at the feast, she was addressing all of us: *Do whatever he tells you*. Like those servants, we must obey God even when He speaks in a way that seems strange to us. They were concerned about wine; Jesus told them to fill water-pots with water. What was the point?, they could rightly have asked. Following Mary's recommendation, they obeyed without query, and they filled the water-pots to the brim. Mary's intercession and those servants' docility obtained the miracle.

Devotion to saints and to relics

And God did miracles through Paul's hand, that were beyond all wont; so much so, that when handkerchiefs or aprons which had touched his body were taken to the sick, they got rid of their diseases, and evil spirits were driven out (Acts 19:11-12).

The Acts of the Apostles show us many instances of the spiritual power of the saints, even when these are still pilgrims on earth. The Apostles and deacons were given a share in God's own power; Peter, John, Stephen, Philip, were able to perform miracles. When a Christian woman called Tabitha, or Dorcas, died in Joppa, the disciples asked Peter to come. They did not ask God directly for a miracle; when Peter came *they took him into the upper room, where all the widows stood round him in tears, showing him the coats and cloaks which Dorcas used to make while she was among them* (Acts 9:39). They left everything in Peter's hands. Peter did not tell them to pray for a miracle; he sent them all out *and went on his knees to pray; then, turning to the body, he said, Tabitha, rise up; and she opened her eyes and looked at Peter, and sat up on the bed. So he gave her his hand, and raised her to her feet; and then, calling in the saints and the widows, he showed her to them alive* (Acts 9:40-41).

We read in the Acts of the Apostles that people *even used to bring sick folk into the streets, and lay them down there on beds and pallets, in the hope that even the shadow of Peter, as he passed by, might fall upon one of them here and there, and so they would be healed of their infirmities. From neighbouring cities, too, the common people flocked to Jerusalem, bringing with them the sick and those who were troubled by unclean spirits; and all of them were cured* (Acts 5:15-16). Peter was a good instrument in the hands of God, and so are all the saints. Such was the power at work in Peter, that even his shadow could bring about miracles.

Does such devotion to saints take away the glory due to God? Certainly not. Both Peter and Paul made it clear that their power came from God, not from themselves. Their attitude was totally opposed to that of King Herod, whom God struck dead for letting men worship him as a god: *the people cried out in applause, It is no man, it is a god that speaks. And immediately the angel of the Lord smote him, for not referring the glory to God; and he was eaten up by worms, and so died* (Acts 12:22-23).

What a contrast when we look at the Apostles! When Peter and John cured a lame man near the Temple Gate, *all the crowd gathered about them in what is called Solomon's Porch, beside themselves with wonder. Peter, when he saw it, addressed himself to the people; Men of Israel, he said, why does this astonish you? Why do you fasten your eyes on us, as if we had enabled him to walk through some power or virtue of our own? It is the God of Abraham and Isaac and Jacob, the God or our fore-fathers, who has thus brought honour to His Son Jesus* (Acts 3:12-13).

In Lystra, when Paul cured a man crippled from birth, *the multitudes, seeing what Paul had done, cried out in the Lycaonian dialect, It is the gods, who have come down to us in human shape. They called Barnabas Jupiter, and Paul Mercury, because he was the chief speaker, and the priest of Jupiter, Defender of the City, brought out bulls and wreaths to the gates, eager, like the multitude, to do sacrifice. The apostles tore their garments when they heard of it; and both Barnabas and Paul ran out among the multitude, crying aloud: Sirs, why are you doing all this? We too are mortal men like yourselves; the whole burden of our preaching is that you must turn away from follies like this to the worship of the living God, who made sky and earth and sea and all that is in them* (Acts 14:10-14).

The Saints did not allow themselves to be worshipped like God. Yet they did not chase away

those who came to them asking for miracles. In
accordance with His promise, God granted many
favours through their intercession. The power of the
Saints is not diminished, on the contrary, by their entry
into eternal glory. Once they are in Heaven, they are
even more perfect, more pleasing to God, who does not
refuse the requests of His faithful friends. We know
that the saints in Heaven take an interest in what is
happening on earth, for Christ said, speaking of the
man who had found his lost sheep and rejoiced: *So it
is, I tell you, in heaven; there will be more rejoicing over
one sinner who repents, than over ninety-nine souls that
are justified, and have no need of repentance* (Luke
15:7). So we can turn to the saints in Heaven, those
great friends of God, asking them to pray for us. It is
God's will that His saints should be known and set as
an example for others to follow: *and your light must
shine so brightly before men that they can see your good
works, and glorify your Father who is in heaven* (Matt.
5:16). When we honour the saints, we give glory to God
who sanctified them and worked wonders in them.

Not only does the Bible testify that devotion to the
saints is pleasing to God, but it also lays the foundation
for the honour rendered to relics, i.e. objects that are
somehow related to Christ Himself or to saints.

What special power could the cloak of Jesus
possess? It was only a piece of cloth! Yet we read in the
Gospel that *a woman who for twelve years had been
troubled with an issue of blood, came up behind him
and touched the hem of his cloak; she said to herself, If I
can even touch the hem of his cloak, I shall be healed*
(Matt. 9:20-21). St. Luke, who was himself a doctor,
tells us in detail what happened. *Jesus said, Who*

touched me? All disclaimed it; Master, said Peter and his companions, the multitudes are hemming thee in and crowding upon thee, and canst thou ask, Who touched me? But Jesus said, Somebody touched me; I can tell that power has gone out from me. And the woman, finding that there was no concealment, came forward trembling and fell at his feet, and so told him before all the people of her reason for touching him, and of her sudden cure (Luke 8:45-47). Jesus' cloak, because it belonged to Him, could be an instrument of divine power. Evidently the woman did not worship the cloak, but Christ who was its owner.

Yes, the power of God can reach us through creatures, even through mere objects that have been in contact with the body of a holy person. We cannot deny it, for the Bible tells us so: such was the fame of holiness of St. Paul in Ephesus that all flocked to him and those who were not able to approach him would obtain from a more fortunate person some piece of cloth that had touched him, because *when handkerchiefs or aprons which had touched his body were taken to the sick, they got rid of their diseases, and evil spirits were driven out* (Acts 19:12).

Such attitude was obviously not a case of idolatry, or God would not have sanctioned it by miracles, which are the seal of His approval. The honour given to relics is a relative honour, i.e. a manifestation of the honour due to Christ or to God's friends. It does not rob God of the glory due to Him; on the contrary, it leads us to glorify God by acknowledging the wonders God worked in the souls of the saints.

To Jesus through Mary

> *Going into the dwelling, they found the child there, with his mother Mary, and fell down to worship him* (Matt. 2:11).

The whole purpose of Mary's life was to bring Christ to men. He received His body from her, she gave birth to Him and looked after Him. Far from being an obstacle between Christ and Christians, she is a link of union, and the Holy Spirit, author of Sacred Scripture, lets us get a glimpse of it in the pages of the Gospels.

When did Jesus and John the Baptist meet for the first time? On the banks of the Jordan? No. They met in a town of Juda, in the hill country where his parents lived. When Mary went to visit her cousin Elizabeth who was expecting a baby in her old age, she brought Christ to the mother and her child. *No sooner had Elizabeth heard Mary's greeting than the child leaped in her womb; and Elizabeth herself was filled with the Holy Ghost; so that she cried out with a loud voice, Blessed art thou among women, and blessed is the fruit of thy womb. How have I deserved to be thus visited by the mother of my Lord? Why, as soon as ever the voice of thy greeting sounded in my ears, the child in my womb leaped for joy. Blessed art thou for thy believing; the message that was brought to thee from the Lord shall have fulfilment* (Luke 1:41-45). Thanks to Mary's presence, John the Baptist was sanctified in his mother's womb.

When the shepherds came looking for the new-born Saviour announced by Angels, they found *Mary and Joseph there, with the child lying in the manger* (Luke 2:16). The child was with Mary, *and the shepherds went home giving praise and glory to God, at seeing and hearing that all was as it had been told them* (Luke 2:20).

Forty days later, Simeon also met Jesus in His mother's arms: *When the child Jesus was brought in by his parents, to perform the custom which the law enjoined concerning him, Simeon too was able to take him in his arms. And he said, blessing God: Ruler of all, now dost thou let thy servant go in peace, according to thy word; for my own eyes have seen that saving power of thine which thou hast prepared in the sight of all nations. This is the light which shall give revelation to the Gentiles, this is the glory of thy people Israel* (Luke 2:27-32). The prophetess Ana, arriving at that very moment, *came near to give God thanks, and spoke of the child to all that patiently waited for the deliverance of Israel* (Luke 2:38).

Following the star that led them to Bethlehem, the Magi were seeking the new-born King of Israel. *Going into the dwelling, they found the child there, with his mother Mary, and fell down to worship him; and, opening their stores of treasures, they offered him gifts, of gold and frankincense and myrrh* (Matt. 2:11).

All those who meet Mary are seen and heard glorifying God. To meet Mary is to find Christ, and Christ leads us to God the Father.

Mary brought Christ to us. She also wants to take us closer to Him. She teaches us only one lesson through her example and through her words: humble and wholehearted obedience to God's will. Apart from her *magnificat*, which is a beautiful hymn of praise and thanksgiving, and the episode of the finding of the Child Jesus in the Temple, when Mary expresses her anguish in a trusting, humble reproach to her Son who is also her God, the Gospels quote her words only on two occasions: the Anunciation and the wedding-feast in Cana of Galilee. *Behold the handmaid of the Lord; let it be unto me according to thy word* (Luke 1:38): an act of perfect submission to God's plans for her. *Do whatever he tells you* (John 2:5): she advises us to pay attention to Christ and heed His words. Indeed, when we find Mary, it does not take us long to be close to God.

Following the teachings of the Bible, we should seek the help of our Mother, Christ's Mother. Her Son does not deny any of her petitions, and let us never forget that, by honouring her, we pay homage to her divine Son, and we give glory to God, who wrought for her His wonders (cf. Luke 1:49).

Conclusion

The Church which we have been contemplating in the pages of the Bible is still fundamentally the same today. Led by Jesus Christ who speaks and acts through His representatives on earth (the Pope and the Bishops), the Church continues proclaiming faithfully God's message of salvation.

While others have succumbed to the pressures of a paganised modern society, the Catholic Church remains firm in upholding Christian principles. The Bride of Christ raises Her voice in defence of the sacred character of human life at all stages of development, of the unity and indissolubility of Marriage, of the true nature of Holy Orders; conscious of Her responsibility before God, She refuses to lower the high ideals offered us by Christ. Thanks to the tireless and often heroic dedication of many holy successors of St. Peter assisted by the Holy Spirit, all can hear the voice of Christ and find the right path that leads to Life.

The Church is always sanctifying men through the grace of God flowing from the seven Sacraments, identical now to what they were when Christ instituted them and the Apostles administered them in the 1st century of Christianity: Baptism, Confirmation, Holy Eucharist, Penance, Anointing of the Sick, Holy Orders and Matrimony.

Only in the Catholic Church are all Christ's teachings preserved and obeyed. Only there are all the teachings of the Bible followed and adhered to, without any sort of compromise.

I am astounded that you should be so quick to desert one who called you to the grace of Christ, and go over to another Gospel; this can only mean that certain people are causing disquiet among you, in their eagerness to pervert the Gospel of Christ. Friends, though it were we ourselves, though it were an angel from heaven that should preach to you a gospel other than the gospel we preached to you, a curse upon him! I repeat now the warning we gave you before it happened, if anyone preaches to you what is contrary to the tradition you received, a curse upon him (Gal. 1:6-9).

Christians of non-Catholic denominations follow no Tradition. Tradition is, by definition, the passing down of opinions, beliefs, practices, customs etc., from the past to the present, especially by word of mouth or practice; and the body of principles, beliefs, practices, experience etc. passed down from the past to the present. In their own words and according to their own testimony, Christians of non-Catholic denominations acknowledge one authority only, the Bible, following the principle of *sola scriptura* (*nothing except the Bible*). Forgetting that Christ's teachings were transmitted mainly by word of mouth, they eventually accepted interpretations of the Bible that went against the Tradition received by the first Christians from the

Apostles who were proclaiming the message of Christ. They first of all rejected the authority of the Pope, successor of St. Peter and holder of the Keys; then, left on their own, they were victims of the dangers of private interpretation of the Bible which St. Peter had warned against, when making reference to the Epistles of St. Paul: *there are passages in them difficult to understand, and these, like the rest of scripture, are twisted into a wrong sense by ignorant and restless minds, to their own undoing* (2 Peter 3:16). Consequently they lost a great part of Christian Tradition, including infant Baptism, auricular and secret Confession of sins, Real Presence of Jesus Christ in the consecrated Bread and Wine, Anointing of the Sick, consecration of priests with divine power to speak and act in the Person of Christ, celebration of Matrimony as a Sacrament, devotion to the Mother of God, Angels and Saints.

The Catholic Church has been faithful to the Tradition passed down throughout the centuries, in obedience to St. Paul's recommendation: *(God) has called you, through our preaching, to attain the glory of our Lord Jesus Christ. Stand firm, then, brethren, and hold by the traditions you have learned, in word or in writing, from us. So may our Lord Jesus Christ himself, so may God, our Father, who has shown such love to us, giving us unfailing comfort and welcome hope through his grace, encourage your hearts, and confirm you in every right habit of action and speech* (2 Thess. 2:13-16).

As we have seen in the course of this study, a substantial part of Christian Tradition is expressed, or at least reflected, in the pages of the Bible. Let every Christian accept it wholeheartedly, and live by it, and thereby be filled with God's grace and confirmed, as St. Paul said, in every right habit of action and speech. For indifference to Christian Tradition leads necessarily, we have seen it, to a distortion of the Bible's teachings.

Appendix One

Jewish, Catholic and Protestant versions of the Bible

What is the difference?

Old Testament

The Jewish Bible is made up exclusively of Old Testament Books. The first books to be accepted as inspired were those of the Law (Genesis, Exodus, Leviticus, Numbers, Deuteronomy). Gradually other writings were accepted because they assured the faithful practice of the Law. Finally, as the Christian era dawned, the sacred writings had become a definite collection whose contents could not be modified.

Beside the Palestinian Jews, there was a large community of Greek-speaking Jews whose principal centre was at Alexandria. For their benefit, a Greek translation of the Old Testament was made, known as the Septuagint. This Greek version included additional books and passages not found in the original Hebrew text. It appears that the Palestinian Jews had a stricter notion of inspiration than their Hellenistic brothers. However, some of those texts were used in Palestinian synagogues; Ecclesiasticus, to give only one example, was held in high esteem and was frequently quoted in rabbinical literature.

As the Apostles went preaching everywhere and Christians multiplied all over the Roman Empire, they made use of the Greek version of the Old Testament, the Septuagint, which was the one read in the Jewish synagogues.

After the destruction of Jerusalem towards the end of the 1st century, the Palestinian Jews, anxious to preserve their cultural heritage and to avoid Christian *contamination*, made an official list of sacred writings at the Synod of Jamnia, A.D. 90-100.

The criteria of selection were the following:

1) conformity with the Law of Moses

2) antiquity (the time of writing could not be later than the time of Esdras)

3) Hebrew language

4) Palestinian origin.

The Books contained exclusively in the Septuagint did not satisfy all those requirements and were therefore excluded from the official Hebrew Bible. Wisdom and 2 Machabees, for instance, were written in Greek; Ecclesiasticus and 1 Machabees, after the time of Esdras; Baruch, outside Palestine.

It is interesting to note that this selection was the result of a nationalistic attitude, coupled with a certain lack of faith. It was not reasonable to set arbitrary restrictions to God's Revelation. Why should God stop speaking at the time of Esdras, when the promised Saviour had not yet come? Why should He speak only in Hebrew, and only to Palestinian Jews?

And so Christians continued the practice of the Apostles, who made abundant use of the Septuagint in their preaching. This is why the Catholic Old Testament includes Tobias, Judith, Wisdom, Ecclesiasticus, Baruch, 1 & 2 Machabees and certain parts of Esther and Daniel not to be found in the Hebrew version. It is, however, on the authority of the Church, not on any Jewish authority, that the list of inspired Old Testament books was drawn.

Sixteen centuries after Christ, the Protestants questioned the traditional biblical texts and decided 'to go back to the sources', adopting the Hebrew Old Testament. What the Protestants actually did was to draw their water, the word of God preparing the coming of Christ, from a source motivated by anti-Christian feelings.

The Catholics, on the other hand, continued drinking from the source indicated to them by the Apostles guided by the Holy Spirit.

New Testament

The list of Books which now form the New Testament was formed gradually. It was determined by the authority of the Apostles and made known to successive generations through the oral Tradition of the Church.

With the rise of Protestantism, Luther did try to eliminate the Epistle of St. James, because it so blatantly contradicted his teachings; however, he did not succeed. Nowadays, the Protestant New Testament is made up of the Books which Catholic Tradition holds as inspired. The difference resides in the trustworthiness of the translation and explanatory footnotes.

Appendix Two

Recommended Bibliography

Catholic Doctrine in General

The Faith Explained, Leo Trese, Sinag-Tala
The Catholic Catechism, John A. Hardon, Doubleday & Co.
Catechism of the Council of Trent, Marian Publications
Basic Christian Doctrine, J. M. Cavanna, Vera-Reyes
Apologetics, Monsignor Paul J. Glenn, Tan Books & Publishers
A Catholic Commentary on Holy Scripture, Thomas Nelson and Sons Ltd.
Fundamentals of Catholic Dogma, Dr. Ludwig Ott, Tan Books & Publishers

Selected topics

Marriage: A Path to Sanctity, J. Abad and E Fenoy, Sinag-Tala
Mary of Nazareth, Federico Suarez, Scepter
Simon Peter, Monsignor Georges Chevrot, Sinag-Tala
Joseph of Nazareth, Federico Suarez, Scepter

About being a Priest, Federico Suarez, Four-Courts Press

The Catholic Church through the Ages, Martin P. Harney, St. Paul Editions

A Short History of the Catholic Church, Jose Orlandis, Four-Courts Press

Evidence for our Faith, Joseph H. Cavanaugh, University of Notre-Dame Press, Burns, Oates & Macmillan Inc.

Christian Life

Writings of the Venerable Josemaría Escrivá:
The Way
Furrow
The Forge
Christ is passing by
Friends of God
In Love with the Church
The Way of the Cross
Holy Rosary

Bible

The New Testament of Our Lord and Saviour Jesus Christ, translated by Monsignor Ronald Knox, Burns and Oates, Publishers to the Holy See, London

The Holy Bible, Ronald Knox version, Burns, Oates & Macmillan Inc.

The Holy Bible, Douay-Rheims version, Tan Publishers

The Holy Bible, Revised Standard Version Catholic Edition, Oxford University Press, Oxford.

The Navarre Bible, Four Courts Press, Dublin